Storrs Lectures
on Jurisprudence
Yale Law School, 1988

THE
FACES
OF
INJUSTICE

JUDITH N. SHKLAR

YALE UNIVERSITY PRESS
NEW HAVEN AND LONDON

Published with assistance from the foundation established
in memory of Philip Hamilton McMillan of the
Class of 1894, Yale College.

Material from Judith N. Shklar's "Giving Injustice Its Due" is
reprinted by permission of The Yale Law Journal Company and
Fred B. Rothman & Company from *The Yale Law Journal
Company*, vol. *98, 1135–51*.

Designed by Jill Breitbarth.
Set in Palatino type by
Marathon Typography Service, Inc., Durham, North Carolina.
Printed in the United States of America by
Edwards Brothers, Inc., Ann Arbor, Michigan.

Library of Congress Cataloging-in-Publication Data
Shklar, Judith N.
The faces of injustice / Judith N. Shklar.
p.   cm. — (Storrs lectures on jurisprudence ; 1988)
Includes bibliographical references.
ISBN 0-300-04599-9 (alk. paper)
1. Justice. 2. Justice, Administration of—United States.
I. Title. II. Series.
K240.S47   1990
340'.11—dc20   89-21463
                                                CIP

The paper in this book meets the guidelines for permanence
and durability of the Committee on Production Guidelines for
Book Longevity of the Council on Library Resources.

10 9 8 7 6 5 4 3 2 1

CONTENTS

PREFACE

This book had its beginning in the Storrs Lectures that I gave at the Yale Law School in 1988. I am grateful to Dean Guido Calabresi for having invited me and for making it such a pleasant occasion. I learned a lot from talking to the students and faculty at Yale and appreciated their kindness and hospitality. I am also much obliged to Professor Sanford Kadish, who asked me to discuss the original lectures with a workshop at the Boalt Hall Law School at Berkeley, a session from which I benefited greatly. At various times I have also presented sections of this book to informal groups at Harvard, and I found that each one of them helped me to put my ideas in order.

Geoffrey Hawthorn, Stephen Holmes, Quentin Skinner, and Dennis Thompson read earlier drafts of this book with real care and gave me much excellent and detailed advice about how to improve it, almost all of which I was happy to accept. To say thank you to them is hardly enough. I also received valuable comments from Yaron Ezrahi, Moshe Halbertal, Stanley Hoffmann, George Kateb, Robert Keohane, Steven Macedo, Patrick Riley, and Michael Walzer. Heather Houlahan kindly helped me to prepare the manuscript for publication.

An earlier and shorter version of the first chapter of this book appeared in the *Yale Law Journal*, June 1989.

THE

FACES

OF

INJUSTICE

INTRODUCTION

When is a disaster a misfortune and when is it an injustice? Intuitively the answer seems quite obvious. If the dreadful event is caused by the external forces of nature, it is a misfortune and we must resign ourselves to our suffering. Should, however, some ill-intentioned agent, human or supernatural, have brought it about, then it is an injustice and we may express indignation and outrage. As it happens, in actual experience this distinction, to which we cling so fervently, does not mean very much. The reasons become clear enough when we recall that what is treated as unavoidable and natural, and what is regarded as controllable and social, is often a matter of technology and of ideology or interpretation. The perceptions of victims and of those who, however remotely, might be victimizers, tend to be quite different. Neither the facts nor their meaning will be experienced in the same way by the afflicted as by mere observers or by those who might have averted or mitigated the suffering. These people are too far apart to see things in the same way.

Nor is the line between the human and the natural altogether relevant. Culture, in its pervasiveness, may act upon us in much the same way as the natural environment does, and it is certainly

1

no easier—indeed it may be harder—to control and alter. The most obvious example is pigmentation, which is certainly natural, but nothing else about being dark-skinned in America is. Black in America is a social, not a natural condition. And at various times some have regarded dark skin as a misfortune, some always knew it to be an injustice, and not a few treated it as both. With that in mind, it would seem that the line between human and nonhuman causes may not matter very much.[1] Instead, I shall argue, the difference between misfortune and injustice frequently involves our willingness and our capacity to act or not to act on behalf of the victims, to blame or to absolve, to help, mitigate, and compensate, or to just turn away. The notion that there is a simple and stable rule to separate the two is a demand for a moral security, which like so many others, cannot be satisfied. That does not mean that we should abolish the distinction or become resigned to all our ills, but it does suggest that we should reconsider it and, especially, take a new look at injustice.

An earthquake is surely a natural event, but that is not all that can or will in fact be said about it if a lot of damage is done and many people perish. It will be considered an injustice as well and for some quite different reasons. The religious will blame God. "Why us?" they will cry out. "We are not more wicked than other towns, why single us out for punishment?" And even more specifically, "why my child?" Among the less devout victims, a few might simply say, "nature is cruel," but they would not be numerous, because a random, arbitrary world is hard to bear, and the desolate will begin to look around for some responsible human agents. And they might find them soon enough. There are bound to be many people who did contribute to the catastrophe and made its impact worse. Many buildings do collapse because contractors have violated construction codes and bribed inspectors. The population is rarely fully warned of these dangers, which technologically sophisticated devices can often predict. Public authorities, moreover, may not always make serious preparations for the eventuality. There would be no effectively organized emergency measures, no adequate medical relief and no swift transportation for the injured. Many will die who might have been saved. Where had their taxes gone to? Squandered on an expensive space program that was of no particular benefit to them, they might say.

While this is an imaginary case, it bears a certain resemblance to the recent earthquake in Armenia, but something less extreme is not unimaginable in any part of the world. I have only slightly exaggerated the prevalence of simple, active injustice here, committed by crooks and corrupt officials. No one would try to exonerate them, and, indeed, politicians will hasten to heap blame upon them. The less culpable governmental agents, who might well be accused of neglecting the victims by simply following routine, would, however, stress that this was a natural and unavoidable disaster and that, given the many other demands upon their limited resources, they had done their best, and more. To the cry, "why us?" they would say, "life's unfair," which is also the favorite evasion of passively unjust citizens, the people who just stand around and do nothing, calm in the belief that "it could not be helped." The victims would not have accepted excuses of "necessity" and inevitability. They would have seen injustice and cried out in anger and they would have been quite right to do so, because there was a human, political element in the disaster. And in a free, constitutional democracy especially, in which public authorities are supposed to be responsive and accountable to the taxpayers, the outrage of the victims on such dramatic occasions is right in itself, as well as being a contribution to the public good, since it might improve official conduct when the next disaster occurs. From the point of view of the victims and those who sympathize with them, what began as a natural disaster was in its full effects a public injustice. Given their expectations of current technology and belief in political equality, these citizens would and should vent their outrage upon the established authorities in the hope of at least making them more efficient and careful and less arrogant now and in the future.

To take the victims' views seriously, does not, however, mean that they are always right when they perceive injustice. We often blame ourselves and each other for no good reason. We scapegoat, we accuse wildly, we feel guilty for acts we never performed, we blame anyone who seems more fortunate than ourselves. When a child dies of a fatal disease, it may not be the fault of God, of the doctors, of our parents whose genes we inherited, or our own past actions, but most of us will blame one or all of these. It really is just a misfortune, even if it is the worst thing that could happen to us. To cast blame may offer some much needed relief, but it is unjust, though hardly blameworthy.

Indeed, there are times when it seems that Americans especially are engaged in no other sport than in blaming each other, because we have such high social and technological expectations. It has been said that we demand nothing less than "total justice."[2] Even worse is the very common impulse to seek out conspiracies where none are to be found. Would we not be better off if we learned to accept the burdens of inevitability, both social and natural? It may be true that wrongdoing by private and public organizations can sooner or later be pinned on some guilty persons, that "many hands" are not invisible or powerless members of a corporate entity who must be absolved from blame, but it is not true that everything terrible that is caused by human beings is really any specific person's fault. A lot of very minor, innocent errors can add up to a major technological or military failure.[3] Not only the legacies of the past, but technological error, misunderstanding, confusion, and operational failure all combine to lead to awful human-generated disasters, but no one can really be personally identified as deserving to be blamed for them. Certainly there is no intent to harm or dereliction of normal duty. We ought, perhaps, not to cry injustice quite so readily. It might make life easier all around. That is not a proposition that would appeal to the victims of this world, and from their vantage point, it might make more sense to forget about the idea of misfortune. They might be more interested in guilt specifically, even if many hands were at work in bringing about their plight.

Should we, then, cease to make the distinction between misfortune and injustice since it makes so little sense, except as a

way of rationalizing our reactions to potential and actual disasters? I do not see how we could ever do that. Surely it is psychologically unthinkable that we could ever desist from casting blame
upon those who have injured us and who have disappointed our
social expectations. How could we accept a ruleless world in which
things just happened to us? Even blaming oneself is more tolerable than folding up in front of so absurd a life. As long as we have
a sense of injustice, we will want not only to understand the
forces that cause us pain but also to hold them responsible for
it—if we can identify them. How punitive we should be is quite
another question, and it would take an additional book to consider it adequately.

To be sure, the objects of our suspicions do constantly alter.
We no longer blame witches for our personal misfortunes, as we
did until a few centuries ago. Some misfortunes of the past, however, are now injustices, such as infant mortality and famines,
which are caused mainly by public corruption and indifference.
Nevertheless, though it is undoubtedly changeable and indefi-
nite, the difference between misfortune and injustice will not go
away, and there are good public reasons why we should retain
it. We need it not only to make sense of our experiences but
also to control and restrain the public sources of danger to our
safety and security. But we must recognize that the line of separa-
tion between injustice and misfortune is a political choice, not a
simple rule that can be taken as a given. The question is, thus,
not whether to draw a line between them at all, but where to do
so in order both to enhance responsibility and to avoid random
retaliation.

Accusations of injustice are often the sole resort open, not only
to the victims, but to all citizens who have an interest in maintaining high standards of public service and rectitude. They can
also discourage passive injustice, which is the refusal of both
officials and of private citizens to prevent acts of wrongdoing when
they could and should do so. It is a notion as old as Cicero that
challenges most of us, who would prefer to do nothing, by reminding us that we may, in effect, be contributing to injustices. Not

everything that afflicts victims is just bad luck, and alert citizens and officials can do much to alleviate and prevent injustice.

By passive injustice I do not mean our habitual indifference to the misery of others, but a far more limited and specifically civic failure to stop private and public acts of injustice. The possibility of such preventive civic activity is by far greater in a free society than in fear-ridden and authoritarian ones, so I shall treat it as an aspect of the obligation of citizens of constitutional democracies only. And, indeed, although I shall draw examples from many places and times, this whole book is really about America, not because it is the most unjust society by any means, but because I know it best and because one might as well point one's finger at one's own country when one writes about injustice. It is in America, moreover, that the character of citizenship has always been, and remains, a matter of daily discussion. As citizens, we are passively unjust, I shall argue, when we do not report crimes, when we look the other way when we see cheating and minor thefts, when we tolerate political corruption, and when we silently accept laws that we regard as unjust, unwise, or cruel.

Public servants are even more likely to be passively unjust, being by training unwilling to step outside the rules and routines of their offices and peers, afraid to antagonize their superiors or to make themselves unduly conspicuous. The resulting injustice is not due to natural forces nor to a particularly unjust system, but to many hands in general, who need to be reminded constantly of the possible consequences of their inaction. Many social workers and doctors knew that little Joshua DeShaney's father was beating him brutally. His final caseworker "dutifully recorded these incidents in her files . . . but she did nothing more," with the result that he is now permanently brain damaged. The state, the U.S. Supreme Court held, could not be held responsible for Joshua's end under the Due Process Clause of the Constitution, but Justice William Brennan is hardly alone in thinking that doing nothing under such circumstances amounts to as great an injustice as any that a modern state can commit.[4]

Nevertheless, one could say that the child was the victim of a misfortune, first to have such a father, then to fall through the cracks—to use a fittingly impersonal metaphor—of the system. One might go on to argue that no state has any business to interfere in any family, even this one, since the relations within it are a wholly private matter. In truth, the line separating the private from the public sphere is even more uncertain than the one drawn between misfortunes and injustices. This, too, is a political choice, depending on ideology and deep cultural habits of mind. Need one recall that until very recently it was generally taken for granted that a white primary was a private arrangement? Anyone who thought otherwise was giving way to *subjective* personal attitudes.

Any free citizen must insist that a line be drawn somewhere between the private and the public so that the state will be prohibited from entering into the many aspects of our lives where we have the right to act as we choose. The exact point of its exclusion is, however, historically movable, and few are the liberals who would now treat domestic violence against women and children as a protected private sphere. The way to decide when an injustice is so evident as to require citizens and officials to interfere cannot, however, be found in the difference between publicly recognized injustices and merely subjective reactions. That distinction is, in fact, no more secure, and no less political, than that between nature and culture or between the objective and the subjective view. It is a question of who has the power to define the meaning of actions.

What usually passes for validated injustice is an act that goes against some known legal or ethical rule. Only a victim whose complaints match the rule-governed prohibitions has suffered an injustice. If there is no fit, it is only a matter of the victim's subjective reactions, a misfortune, and not *really* unjust. She may not be lying or mistaken about the facts, though that is to be suspected, but she has misdefined her experience. Her expectations were groundless. Not only does this procedure miss a good deal about what it is like to suffer injustice, it also assumes a stability of perspectives that is just not there. Who exactly is to decide what does and what does not constitute a valid expecta-

tion? The law of contracts may do so well enough for the relations it is designed to cover, but there are a lot of unjust relations
out there that have nothing to do with contracts or bilateral
promises.

Let us assume that the victim's expectations may not have been
recognized as valid by those whom he or she accuses or by the
proverbial impartial observer. They may soon be regarded as very
just indeed and may already have been looked upon as such by
some of her or his fellow citizens. In 1930 a vast amount of
scientific eugenics in effect underwrote Jim Crow laws. To have
claimed that black American citizens might expect to have exactly
the same rights as white citizens would have appeared as an
unfounded expectation, an expression of a subjective sense of
injustice. Yesterday's rock solid rule is today's folly and bigotry.
Nor is social change the only reason for skepticism about normal
judgments. The reports of witnesses to accidents, the psychology of perceptions, and the impact of personal and public ideologies upon our interpretive faculties all tell the same story, and it is
well known. Yet we still pretend that there must be one true
account to tell us what *really* happened and whether a disaster
was a misfortune or an injustice. We need to believe this, obviously, for deep psychological reasons, but not because we cannot
act without certain knowledge. We do it all the time, after all,
because we must. That is why many skeptics have noted that the
"parajudicial conception of morality" leaves much to be desired
because it does not correspond to our daily experience of moral
and political choice and conflict.[5]

There is no denying that the parajudicial model has been the
normally accepted one. To the skeptic it has, however, always
seemed to be feeble because it assumes that we know more about
each other and about social control than we in fact do or can ever
hope to know. For a variety of reasons, that was certainly what
Plato, Augustine, and Montaigne thought, and I shall begin this
book by recalling their doubts, which I share. My argument will,
however, be more modest and more political than theirs. I shall
simply try to show that none of the usual models of justice offer

an adequate account of injustice because they cling to the groundless belief that we can know and draw a stable and rigid distinction between the unjust and the unfortunate. Moreover, this belief
inclines us to ignore passive injustice, the victim's sense of injustice, and ultimately the full, complex, and enduring character of
injustice as a social phenomenon.

Consider the celebrated case of *Bardell v. Pickwick*. The facts as
they appear in Dickens's *Pickwick Papers* are as follows. Mr. Pickwick has been renting rooms from the widow Bardell for some
time when he suddenly decides to hire a manservant. Owing to
his utter inability to express himself clearly and simply, he gives
Mrs. Bardell the impression that he is proposing marriage to her
when he was trying to tell her of his new domestic arrangements.
Anyone reading his speech can see at once that she might misinterpret his remarks, especially if the wish was mother to the
thought. She is "a confiding female" and though an excellent
cook, none too bright. In any event, she is so overcome by his
words that she faints into his arms just as his friends enter the
room. They see a highly embarrassing scene and cough discreetly.
As they would duly testify, "She certainly was reclining in his
arms." This is Victorian England and Mrs. Bardell has been com-
promised and so has Pickwick.

Although there are three reliable witnesses who have seen Pickwick embracing Mrs. Bardell, we are the only people who really
know what happened. Dickens and his readers, who like God
have created all these people, are omniscient. We know everything and we are so remote from the events that we can be totally
impartial. This is never possible in real life as the great skeptics
have reminded us all along. As ordinary people we are all in the
same position as Pickwick's and Mrs. Bardell's friends, who have
every reason to believe that it was no accident that she was reclining in his arms. Yet we go right on acting as if we knew as much
about those whom we judge as God does. In the event, it is not
easy to decide who was and who was not unjust, even with all
the unnaturally complete information at our disposal.

Mrs. Bardell's and Pickwick's experience of injustice has hardly begun. Presently, a pair of shyster lawyers, Dodson and Fogg, take on Mrs. Bardell "on spec," or a contingency fee, as it is called in the United States, and she sues Pickwick for breach of promise. The jury hears out Mrs. Bardell and the witnesses to her swoon. On the evidence available to them they could not possibly have decided any other way than to hold for Mrs. Bardell, and she is awarded a considerable sum in damages. We, being omniscient, of course, know that this is an unjust verdict, because Pickwick did not propose to her. But even his friends evidently suspected him, and while Pickwick complains of the "force of circumstances" and "the dreadful conjunction of appearances," his lawyer, Perker, has a point when he notes, "who's to prove it?" We, in our certainty, knowing Pickwick to be innocent, admire his resolve not to pay up and his fortitude in going to jail instead. Not a penny of his will go to line the pockets of Fogg and Dodson, "pettifogging robbers" who have conspired to undo him.

What of Mrs. Bardell? Even the best philosophical treatises on promises would have little to say about her.[6] They would all concentrate entirely on Pickwick's presumed obligations. They are interested solely in his reasons for keeping promises, for being bound tomorrow by something that was said yesterday. They find their answer in society's need for security, in the facilities needed for cooperation among strangers, or in the dictates of a higher law, natural or divine. In theory, the typical promise is a contract, a bilateral agreement of some sort, while gratuitous, unilateral commitments are relegated to the margins of legalistic discourse.[7] The full personal and social implications of broken promises for the person whose expectations have been disappointed are never seriously discussed.

Even the most flexible writers on promising, who see it as one of many relations that entail commitments to others and who recognize the victim's situation, concentrate on the obligations of promising, not on the hopes and trust that may have been aroused, especially in children or in confiding females, for instance.[8] It is as if only the agent, who has some discretionary power, matters. Those who make unilateral promises especially do have something to give, and to that extent they are the stronger of the two parties, and they can potentially abuse their power. From the point of view of the victim, certainly, the broken promise *is* an abuse of power, and that is what makes it unjust. Mrs. Bardell knew that this was exactly what Pickwick had done to her and she was not simply wrong.

If we judge broken promises in terms of the sense of injustice they arouse in the victim and of the intangible damage they may do, then we will not think about them as contracts but as power relations. That is why breaking a gratuitous or casual promise, for example, to take a child to the circus, can be unjust indeed if it is measured by the child's reactions and the influence on the child's character, though it will seem only a minor mistake, such as any parent might carelessly commit, to the impartial observer. At the public level, we should not forget the cynicism that citizens have developed in response to routinely broken official promises. The full cost of broken promises can surely not be counted by an appeal to simple rules of obligation, but only by taking into account the history of the lives that were, like Mrs. Bardell's, disrupted by a sense of injustice.

Was it, after all, just a misfortune that Pickwick was unable to express himself? Had he not in fact trifled with her affections? Is her sense of betrayal and injustice just a subjective reaction? From our vantage point, as God, it may indeed be so, but not from hers or that of her friends. And even we may have no way of coping with her plight. What if the jury had given more weight to Pickwick's age and impeccable character and decided in his favor? Would she have no reason to feel that a huge injustice had been committed? Indeed, can any court do justice to Mrs. Bardell's grievances? She was humiliated in front of a lot of people and nothing can make Pickwick marry her. At most he can be made to pay a sum to the lawyers. Dodson and Fogg no doubt played on Mrs. Bardell's natural desire for revenge, but judicial proceedings cannot really satisfy that urge fully. Had Mrs. Bardell been the heroine of a Gothic romance, she would have put a stiletto through Pickwick's heart and gone mad. And if the story had been set in Corsica, the male members of her clan would have been obliged to avenge her honor by killing Pickwick and his friends who witnessed her disgrace.

Legal justice exists to domesticate, tame, and control all forms of vengeance in the interest of social peace and fairness. However, while civilized living depends upon it, even retributive legal punishment does not and cannot answer the more primitive urges of many victims and their families. Winning the suit may have given Mrs. Bardell a brief satisfaction, but in the end there is no way her sense of injustice could be wholly allayed. Compensatory justice often cannot wipe away the stain of injustice as it is experienced by the victim because more than a broken rule is involved for her. The upshot is that the damage done by some broken promises and by many other injustices cannot be overcome because there is no way to redeem the full loss they cause. That is as true of uncontested instances as of tangled ones like Mrs. Bardell's case.

Until the end, our conventional though truly upright hero, Pickwick, never thinks of Mrs. Bardell, nor of what he might in fact have done to her. He has to have his own education in injustice before he comes to it, but eventually he does.[9] Pickwick in debtor's jail is also suffering an injustice, of course. As we, and only we, know, he never proposed marriage. In time, however, he comes to see that what began as a mishap became a big injustice, for both of them. Both of the parties to this case are victims of injustice in fact. No one in the legal system ever even considered stopping the disastrous course set in motion by Dodson and Fogg. Certainly Pickwick's perfectly decent lawyer, Perker, never tries. For him the judicial proceedings are a game, with its own rules, and he enjoys it, especially since Dodson and Fogg are very skilled players, "capital fellows" according to Perker. It never occurs to him to protest against their sleazy manipulations. When Pickwick calls them a pair of scoundrels, Perker just tells him that he "can't be expected to view these subjects with a professional eye." As a lawyer, his is the insider's view, that of a player within a context of winning and losing. There are many such competitive games, professional, commercial, educational, and political, and they all have rules that determine the conduct of the players, who often do not look beyond the confines of their institutional orders. It is something that has worried every democratic citizen, not least Rousseau: "One can be a devout preacher, a courageous soldier, a dutiful patrician and a bad citizen."[10] That does not mean that their activities are not extremely valuable, in spite of the civic passivity and the injustice to which they are prone. Perker is passively unjust in the most normal and common way, which may even be a good thing, if we choose to tolerate a degree of injustice for the sake of professional cohesion and other socially useful ends.

Perker knows that Dodson and Fogg engage in sharp practices and that imprisonment for debt is wrong, but he does nothing about them. It is not part of being a lawyer. His job is to keep Pickwick out of jail and to get other people in. From Pickwick's point of view, Perker is simply irresponsible. But then, he has had ample occasion to learn about injustice and to discover how inherently unfair imprisonment for debt is. The crooks and the idlers are treated exactly the same as the honest failures, except that the scoundrels do much better in jail than the decent persons, who really suffer. Debtors' prisons were eventually abolished, but no thanks to the Perkers of this world. Pickwick, however, has come to understand the limits of law and conventionality, and so when Mrs. Bardell is also put in jail, because she cannot pay Dodson and Fogg a fee she apparently owes them, he can bear no more. By now his sense of injustice has come into full play and he gives in, pays the lawyers off, and leaves prison, as does Mrs. Bardell. Pickwick is a very decent man and when he sees the new injustice, he does act. Of course, he may have realized by then that he was implicated in Mrs. Bardell's troubles. He and she will no doubt differ for the rest of their lives about what happened to them, but for diverse reasons, they will both know that they were victims of injustice, active as well as passive.

Bardell v. Pickwick is a morality play, not a lawsuit, and I use it here not as comment upon the law but to indicate how very complex the very notion of injustice is. This book has, in fact, no special bearing upon legal justice. My real subject is personal and political injustice and the ways in which we respond to it as agents and especially as victims. Pickwick's and Mrs. Bardell's story is meant to show that it is not enough simply to match the claims of the aggrieved against the rules of justice in order to settle firmly whether she was really treated unjustly or was merely out of luck. If we include the victim's version, not least her sense of injustice, in our understanding of injustice, we might get a far more complete account of its social character. We may find it more difficult to tell an injustice from a misfortune but we might also be less ready to ignore the implications of passive injustice as a part of the full career of human injustice. With these considerations in mind, the sense of injustice should assume a renewed importance, for it is both unfair to ignore personal resentment and imprudent to overlook the political anger in which it finds its expression. Above all, to think about these matters anew might at the very least make the many faces of injustice more visible and more easily recognized.

GIVING

INJUSTICE

ITS DUE

JUSTICE AND INJUSTICE

It will always be easier to see misfortune rather than injustice in the afflictions of other people. Only the victims occasionally do not share the inclination to do so. If, however, we remember that we are all potential victims, we might also decide to reconsider the matter and take a closer and more searching look at injustice—not only at justice—even though this is an unusual enterprise. After all, every courthouse boasts a statue of justice in all her dignity. Justice has been represented in an endless number of pictures.[1] Every volume of moral philosophy contains at least one chapter about justice, and many books are devoted entirely to it. But where is injustice? To be sure, sermons, the drama, and fiction deal with little else, but art and philosophy seem to shun injustice. They take it for granted that injustice is simply the absence of justice, and that once we know what is just, we will know all we need to know. That belief may not, however, be true. One misses a great deal by looking only at justice. The sense of injustice, the difficulties of identifying the victims of injustice, and the many ways in which we all learn to live with each other's injustices tend to be ignored, as is the relation of private injustice to the public order.

15

Why should we not think of those experiences that we call unjust directly, as independent phenomena in their own right? Common sense and history surely tell us that these are common experiences and have an immediate claim on our attention. Indeed, in all likelihood most of us have said, "this is unfair" or "this is unjust" more often than "this is just." Is there nothing much more to be said about the sense of injustice that we know so well when we feel it? Why then do most philosophers refuse to think about injustice as deeply or as subtly as they do about justice? I do not know why a curious division of labor prevails, why philosophy ignores iniquity, while history and fiction deal with little else, but it does leave a gap in our thinking.[2]

Fortunately, political theory, which lives in the territory between history and ethics, seems to me to be ideally suited to do something about it. Injustice is not a politically insignificant notion, after all, and the apparently infinite variety and frequency of acts of injustice invite a style of thought that is less abstract than formal ethics but more analytical than history. At the very least, one might begin to shorten the distance between theory and practice when one looks at our many injustices, rather than only at accounts of what we ought to be and do.

My investigations are not meant to challenge in any way the worth of the various theories of justice, nor their search for its ultimate philosophical foundations. I simply want to consider injustice differently, more directly and in greater depth and detail, and also to illuminate a common condition, victimhood, and especially the sense of injustice that it inspires. Such a project may look less eccentric if we recall that European philosophy features many unconventional intuitions about justice and injustice and that these have often moved the political imagination to its greatest achievements. There are skeptical giants upon whose shoulders I can, with some presumption, try to stand.

What is really involved in the experience of injustice? Of course, the exact meaning of the word *injustice* is "not just" and of *injury*, "not lawful." But is that all that can be said about them? Why should we not think about injustice more amply than simply to note the absence of righteousness? The answer to this question is far from obvious, because the great tradition of ethics would seem to reject this proposal. For there is a normal way of thinking about justice, which Aristotle did not invent but certainly codified and forever imprinted upon all our minds. This normal model of justice does not ignore injustice but it does tend to reduce it to a prelude to or a rejection and breakdown of justice, as if injustice were a surprising abnormality.

The conventional pictorial representation of injustice thus faithfully shows a devil breaking the scales of justice, tearing the blindfold from her eyes, and beating her up.[3] Injustice simply destroys justice. Moreover, although almost all versions of the normal model begin with a brief sketch of injustice, it is clear that it is significant only as the sort of conduct that the rules of justice are designed to control or eliminate. Injustice is mentioned to tell us what must and can be avoided, and once this preliminary task has been quickly accomplished, one can turn with relief to the real business of ethics: justice. I propose to question this program because it does not treat injustice with the intellectual respect it deserves.

At its barest, the normal model argues that any political society is governed by rules. The most primary of these set out the status and entitlements of the members of the polity. This is *distributive justice*, and the rules that it proposes are just if they correspond to the most basic ethical beliefs of the society. In a warrior society, for example, the brave must be rewarded, while in an oligarchy the rich ought to get richer, especially in honors and offices. More abstractly, the fundamental ethos of a polity can be and has been presented as a covenant or as the ensemble of its traditions, ideology, and civil religion. It may be treated as the prompting of nature, reason, and common sense. But in all cases distributive justice depends on something apparently elemental and solid for its authority. Even in a complex modern society in which there may be a multiplicity of belief systems side by side, the normal model reaches down to find some solid ground on which distributive justice can ultimately rest.[4]

Distributive justice is, however, an unfortunate term, partly because it had a very different meaning in the Middle Ages and because it is never clear just what is to be distributed. I shall therefore call it *primary justice*, which is more neutral and merely indicates its place in the normal scheme. In addition to the primary rules settling what is due to whom, there must be effective, specific laws and institutions designed to maintain these rules in the course of private exchanges and to punish those who violate them. And no legal system can be just unless it is managed by officials who are fair, impartial, and committed to the task of maintaining the legal order that gives the society its whole character. When these norms are not followed, there is injustice. Governments that violate them or fail to enforce them are tyrannies, and their subjects may be encouraged to disobey such rulers. That is all that needs to be said: where there is no justice to quell it, injustice prevails.

I do not wish to suggest that there is something absurd about the normal model's construction of justice. It has, after all, been accepted by Aristotelians and Hobbesians, Kantians and utilitarians, liberals and conservatives, and most theologians as well. It corresponds to the common understanding of the matter, in short, and I do not propose to challenge it or to reject the legal values that it promotes. Without juridical institutions and the beliefs that support them, there can be no decent, just, or stable social relations, but only anxiety, mutual mistrust, and insecurity. The state of nature is a perfectly convincing just-so story reminding us of how dismal a nonlegal existence would be. What I do propose to question is not the principle of legality but the normal model's complacent view of injustice and its confidence in the ability of the institutions that it underwrites really to cope with iniquity. Some skeptics have always felt uneasy about these assumptions, and I share their doubts.

No serious theory of justice is simply indifferent to injustice, of course. Normal accounts do begin, as John Stuart Mill's typically does, with the thought that justice, like many other moral notions, is best defined by its opposite. He then goes on to tell us in a very few sentences what injustice involves. It means the violation of good laws, the breaking of promises, the refusal to recognize valid claims, to reward positive merit and to punish crimes, and finally, to be partial in deciding controversies. With that he leaves the subject, having, in fact, shown only that it is unjust to break the rules of normal justice.[5] In this procedure he was by no means unique, but that does not mean that it is a wholly satisfactory one.[6]

Injustice is the absence of justice only in an obvious and circular sense in Mill's account because injustice is presented from the outset as the sort of conduct that normal legal justice is designed to eliminate. To be sure, his real concern was to show why justice is binding upon us and why it is the first of the social virtues. It was not his purpose to draw a full map of all of the kinds of known injustice and their intractability. He was intellectually averse to contemplating the worst historical situations. It was not surprising that, like so many of his successors, he treated injustice merely as the take-off point for a wholesome and upbeat theory of justice. Injustice is not expected to go away, of course, but normal justice is taken implicitly to be adequate to the task of controlling it in practice and understanding it in theory. It is this belief that has often raised skeptical misgivings.

The skeptics do not accuse the normal model of forgetting injustice. They know that laws and conventions are meant to eliminate it. They are not, however, convinced that the normal model offers an elaborate or serious understanding of injustice as a personal and political experience or as a part of all societies known to history. Surely, injustice should not be treated intellectually as a hasty preliminary to the analysis of justice. And the real realm of injustice is not in an amoral and prelegal state of nature. It does not appear only on those rare occasions when a political order wholly collapses. It does not stand outside the gate of even the best of known states. Most injustices occur continuously within the framework of an established polity with an operative system of law, in normal times. Often it is the very people who are supposed to prevent injustice who, in their official capacity, commit the gravest acts of injustice, without much protest from the citizenry.

DOUBTS ABOUT JUSTICE IN THE
EMPIRE OF INJUSTICE

These banal historical realities are the chief reason why there have always been political skeptics who have found the self-confident intellectual and moral claims of the normal model unwarranted. Only Plato rejected it entirely, to be sure. Most of the skeptics accepted the practices of judicial legality as unavoidable, but they had serious doubts about their real worth, and especially about their efficacy. They had taken the full measure of injustice and had found it to be vast.

Political skepticism is often rooted in a general cognitive skepticism, but it does not depend on any specific philosophical assumptions about knowledge in general. It is simply a doubting, unconventional view of accepted social beliefs. This kind of skeptic may well begin the journey away from the common understanding because he or she is overwhelmed by the evil of the times. Certainly Plato, Augustine, and Montaigne had every reason to look about them with despair and disgust. And in the midst of civil war and its debris, it is reasonable to ask: "Why do we do these appalling things?" and then, "What do we know about ourselves and each other?" and finally, "What can we know at all?" That is how the great skeptics came to doubt the moral relevance of the normal model of justice among other things and to reject or question it in ways that made injustice stand out more starkly than conventional political ethics permitted.

It is always the aim of skepticism to expose hidden ignorance. It is not, in fact, difficult to show that laws inspire false intellectual self-assurance that positively encourages us to be unjust. The great skeptics doubted that law-governed conduct could be effective or even possible because we simply cannot know enough about men or events to fulfill its demands. That is why Plato turned his back on the normal model, while Augustine and Montaigne reduced its relevance. All of them had an unusually enlarged sense of the various forms of injustice, and even though they did not focus on the personal sense of injustice, as more democratic theorists eventually would, they gave the theory of injustice its main structure and its intellectual force.

These skeptics did not, of course, deny that lawlessness, crime, and unfairness in exchanges and in judging were acts of wrong-doing, but they looked beyond these obvious misdeeds to redis-cover injustice itself in its scope and endless detail. They saw it directly, not just as encompassing those acts that law and order are meant to eliminate, but all those occasions that make us cry out in anger and resentment: "That is not right!" I evoke their thought here chiefly to show the range of the moral and political puzzles that arise as soon as the normal model is put to a critical test. And if we are prepared to recognize these perplexities, we will be in a better position to take a new look at injustice. The great doubters should help us to raise some questions of our own, and that is why I shall begin this book with their enormous "no!"

Any effort to think about injustice in all its magnitude must begin with Plato, not because he has both the first and the last word on the matter but because he is so remote, so much the foreign mirror in which we learn to see ourselves. To read Plato is to be forced to start all over again because his is the most radical of all rejections of the normal model. There is no other intellectu-ally comparable place to begin.

According to Plato, the normal model is an expression of deep ignorance.[7] It is a bad joke, a circus. Far from altering unjust people, it only encourages and maintains their habits. Injustice, truly understood, is a condition of misdirected psychic energy, in which aggressive and acquisitive impulses expand, while ratio-nality can barely assert itself. A society that reflects this character is not only incapable of educating its members, it, in fact, actively misleads them. Its art of ruling is reduced to keeping these disor-derly tendencies alive by checking them, and with them a mind-less society survives. For what do law courts do but invite the greedy to accuse the even more greedy of offenses arising from greed and aggression? The very existence of the normal model of justice is the most telling testimony to its own incompetence. It not only fails to fulfill its own promise to eliminate injustice, but in its inconsistency does not even try. In our ignorance we invite the unjust to pursue their claims by providing them with public facilities for expressing them.

Can anyone be said to receive or give others what is due, when no one is competent to do his or her assigned task and constantly meddles in affairs that are wholly outside the range of understanding? To Plato it was obvious that all historically known societies are simply unable to achieve their own norms or even to understand them. The reign of ignorance is thus not only inherently disorderly but also unjust in the conventional, normal sense of the word, since no one either gives or receives what is demanded by the normal social rules. If competence and occupation are never matched and there are no ruling principles according to which the inherently unlimited wants of men can be restrained and ordered, there is no justice whatever. The normal model, far from establishing justice, merely allows personal disorder to become socially systemic; it simply perpetuates injustice. Such is its effect and social function.

At its best, law puts injustice into temporary remission. Its failure is not merely in the eye of the observer, Plato, but in its own, given its enormous pretensions. Matters would not be improved, moreover, if the institutions of law enforcement were simply removed from any known society. On the contrary, there might well be greater disorders. The failure of normal justice is, indeed, proved by that likelihood, for it can do nothing to improve the law-abiding citizen. It provides him only with a way of living less dangerously by offering a means to attenuate the consequences of injustice. It does so, however, according to Plato, in a manner that makes the endurance of iniquity inevitable.

Platonic harmony, one might note, is not fairness but then a perfect division of roles and rewards would render conflict so rare as to make normal equity superfluous. The rulers of a rational society do not have to be normally just, though they may choose to be so.[8] Their task is to mold souls and place people in the right social job, which is not the normal form of just government. The latter is, however, utterly self-contradictory in that it aims at justice by positively encouraging injustice. As such it is irrational through and through.

Even a wholly infrarational society would do better than those we know. Here people, rather like pigs, would be prompted by nothing but physical and other immediate needs. The division of labor, production, and consumption would all be limited and ordered by the stringent demands of physical necessity, and there would be no occasion for disorder, for law, or for injustice. When, however, the dominion of need is replaced by that of want, we enter the realm of normal justice, designed merely to check, but in no way to redirect the ways of men perpetually at war with each other, with neighboring cities, and with themselves. Courts, lawyers, assemblies, juries, armies, and all the normal political institutions are merely ways of organizing these disorderly public impulses, which mirror the psychic chaos of individual citizens.

Scarcity and superfluity and their consequences are at the root of normal justice, and all its tendencies enhance them. All this would not go on and on if it were not for moral ignorance, for the inability to understand either our psychic disorder or the structure of public disarray. It is not that people really want matters to be as they are but that they are wholly unable to know themselves and the way to order their lives for happiness. So they settle for the injustices of normal justice, which only freezes them into enduring ignorance.

Unlike the normal model, Plato presents a prelegal state of peace and a juridical nightmare. If his image of the rational order is too difficult to be achieved, it does throw a lurid light on what is usually taken to be justice, which in fact is unjust by its own standards. For normal justice does not and cannot reach its own ends. Neither equal nor proportionate deserts can be distributed when no one even knows what constitutes human worth. No one gets or gives what is owed and no one arrives at the balance, psychic or social, that justice is supposed to establish. That is what ignorance is bound to bring.

For Plato injustice is first and foremost a cognitive problem. Our inability to know the whole and to understand what a rational society would be in its entirety and in every one of its relations renders us incapable of establishing a just order. Even if our knowledge were complete, in all probability we would not be capable of enduring it. One might well infer from Plato's indictment of history that though we have only too clear a notion of injustice, we have never experienced and may not even be able to imagine what justice would be like. Socrates' young friends, in fact, say as much and they do not get much consolation. They are never told what justice is, only under what conditions a rational order might be said to exist. Since we cannot expect to rise to that level, we are left with a searing condemnation of our actual capacities. Ignorance ensures injustice, not only in this or that society, but in all societies, in traditional no less than in consciously self-changing ones.

In a paradoxical attempt to offer a rationally constructed and consistently traditional city, one that was planned really to achieve unchanging customs and beliefs, Plato revealed indirectly that the good old order was as imaginary and as infeasible as the radically rational scheme. Piety, unquestioning faith, the shadow of pollution, and the dangers of offending the gods would require such a mass of regulating officials and educators that one suspects that there are more rulers than ruled in the city of *The Laws*. Normal justice would indeed have its place here, but its validity is limited to punitive functions, which are as necessary to prevent change as they are to uproot any signs of impiety. In the Platonic view, normal justice fails here also because its very necessity proves the collapse of pious, self-enforcing, and terrifying traditions. Law is a poor social medicine because it misunderstands the prior necessity of harmony, whether rational or pious, if injustice is to be overcome. Conventional thinking simply fails to grasp the extent and force of injustice in all possible societies, whether they be traditional or rational, inherited or self-made. Common sense settles for feeble cures because it cannot yield good government. In our ignorance we betray all our hopes, old and new. Plato offers no comfort to conservatives, even if he makes liberals uneasy.

Religious faith is indeed as often at odds with the normal model as is perfect rationality. In European theology, Augustine must always represent the most uncompromising and rigorous vision of the relations between a triumphant and remote God and abjectly sinful and self-destructive humanity. The Augustinian bleakness also has no room for the self-confident implications of most theories of justice. To be sure, there is no Manichaean suggestion that absolute justice and injustice, God and Lucifer, share the governance of the world equally or worse, that evil has triumphed universally over good. There is no doubt about the eventual redemption through Christ, but that has nothing to do with human justice. The condition of sinful men, here and now, is such that law and justice cannot significantly alter their inherited guilt and continuing evil. We would, to be sure, be far more unjust without coercive government and restraints of every sort, but these measures only prevent the worst. And among the consequences of sin is an ignorance so deep that we simply cannot be just, since we can never know enough about each other to make adequate judgments.[9]

The Christian prince or judge trying to be just is doomed to fail. His "lamentable judgments" are grounded in ignorance of the character of the witnesses he tortures and of the accused whom he condemns. We can never know other people well enough to make such decisions rightly, and the more conscientious a judge may be, the more likely he is to deplore the weight of his office. He is, nevertheless, condemned to perform his self-damning duties because without severe punishments everyone would be far worse in every way.[10] The Christian prince may really strive for peace and will at best fight only just wars, but he need not expect to achieve genuine concord either. He, also, is engaging only in damage control, and with the most limited hope of success.

Like Plato, and other skeptics, Augustine recognized injustice as an expression of our limited cognitive resources, but it is a more than pagan ignorance. We do not know enough to give God or man his due. The pagan state cannot know what it owes God and the partially just state that is governed by a Christian ruler also fails in its duty, except possibly in its intentions. And though intentions do make all the difference morally, political actions are always imperfect. Good intentions are not enough to cope with the enormous moral harm that men do in the course of an ordinary day. So justice fails on two grounds, cognitive and practical, and the realm of injustice is revealed to be so extensive that it is quite beyond the cures of even effective political law and order. Evil is so overwhelming that we cannot be just in our sin-created ignorance. In the Augustinian vision injustice embraces more than those social ills that justice might alleviate. It is the sum of our moral failures as sinful people, which from the outset dooms us to being unjust. A Christian ruler will try to do better than a pagan one, but he need expect no great success.

The pagan state exercises only social controls through discipline. Even in Rome at its best everything was done only for the sake of glory. From Augustine's perspective, the proud assertion that the Roman republic had been a just society was more than mere folly; it was a failure to judge the Romans in terms of their real ideology and passions, which were all aimed at war and fame. Cicero, who had claimed that Rome had been a real commonwealth in which each received his due, inevitably became the butt of Augustinian scorn. No grounds could exist for such self-satisfaction in a pagan state, least of all in military Rome. It was not that Cicero, with his love of legal rectitude, was simply wrong but that he had a far too narrow vision of the empire of injustice and the true demands of justice. He was doubly ignorant, first as a man and then as a pagan. It was not, I think, a fair judgment.

Plato and Augustine do not exhaust the skeptical case against the normal model of justice. There is also a purely psychological skepticism that not only doubts that we can ever know enough about each other to devise rules for each other but also suspects that our efforts to do so may do us a lot of harm. Montaigne is the most perfect representative of this line of thought. It seemed to him that we might come to know ourselves, but that others always perceive us differently. Our subjective, personal experiences are too various and incommunicable to be fit into general rules of conduct and the attempt to impose them tends to backfire. Far from reducing our cruelties, rules simply redirect and formalize our ferocity. Moreover, our thoughts and feelings are distorted by the rules of language, our memories are altered by rules of interpretation, and our best moral inclinations are thwarted by social rules. Indeed, no rules that we could invent would be better because we remain both too ignorant and too diverse to be fit into any single normative scheme. We are strangers to one another and we are too ignorant to judge each other.

That is not all. When we trust the rules, we tend to become too sure of our competence and that makes us arrogant, cruel, and tyrannical. In short, the normal model of justice may be entirely unobjectionable, but it is just not made for us. It is not wrong, just futile and deceptive in practice because it ascribes psychological and intellectual qualities to us that we simply do not possess. In our radical uncertainty, therefore, the best we can do is to regret our insuperable limitations and to do as little harm as possible.[11] One might even hope that if we were less eager to judge and condemn, we might have a less violent and fear-ridden society.

This was not Plato's conclusion, but Montaigne's case against the conventions of justice was quite similar to his. In our cognitive poverty we court self-defeat when we believe that our little institutional inventions can cope with our colossal injustice. In fact, they only extend its dominion.

Montaigne's psychological skepticism has lost none of its bite. On the contrary, the findings of contemporary social psychology only reinforce some of his doubts. It appears that very few people are capable of applying statistical information or of making even simple calculations of probability. In making judgments under conditions of less than complete information, most of us therefore misinterpret the evidence available to us. We need statistics and conjectures to make social decisions, but we refuse to accept their mental discipline. The inability to think adequately is, moreover, not a matter of intelligence or education. It is just the way we are. Equally discouraging is our rigidity in altering our beliefs when new information should lead us to change our minds. Our fluency in causal thinking simply allows us to incorporate new evidence without adjusting our previously established expectations. And it also seems that in explaining conduct we tend to attribute our own behavior to external environmental causes but other people's to internal motives.[12] We are intuitively evasive.

Most people are not spontaneous scientists, and common sense is flawed through and through, just as Montaigne thought it was. With that in mind, one might well share his belief that we are unfit for systems of justice, which ignore our psychological and cognitive limitations. The result may therefore be, as he suggested, not only a failure to achieve justice but a general harshness and social rigidity expressing, illusions of adequacy and a false self-assurance. Skepticism here gives injustice its due, because it recognizes that our judgments are made in the dark and doubts that they are right. Such doubt does not have to lead to an all-out Platonic onslaught on our capacities for self-government but it does impose an enhanced sense of the dominion of injustice upon the reflective reader. Indeed, I have begun with a history of skeptical thought for only one purpose: to retrieve the sense it reveals of the enormity of human injustice.

If injustice is as complex and as intractable as seems likely, a less rule-bound phenomenology suggests itself as a better way of exploring the matter. Moreover, once the door to doubt is open, a whole crowd of questions enters one's mind. Among them is a new interest in the victims of injustice, not least because these skeptics make us wonder who the victims really are. Are we not all victims of ignorance? How do we sort victims out? Perhaps the unjust person is the prime victim of his or her own misdeeds. What do we owe to the unjust as well as to their direct victims? How, indeed, are we to recognize the victims of injustice at all?

WHO ARE THE VICTIMS OF INJUSTICE?
THE UNJUST OR THEIR PREY?

If Aristotle is to be our guide, the unjust person is no victim of any kind. He is dominated by only one vice, greed. That is why he breaks the rules of law and fairness. He just wants more of everything, material goods, prestige, and power. And the impact of his greed falls entirely upon others, who receive less than they deserve thanks to his grasping conduct.

The unjust person may, however, first and foremost be unjust to himself by inflicting permanent injuries upon his own soul. This was certainly Plato's view, because he thought that unjust people did not really understand what they were up to, did not act voluntarily, and were usually so misguided that they really deserved pity. They suffer from disordered psyches and are tormented by driving desires and rages that they are unable to satisfy or control. Irrationality, insolence, uncontrollable desires, aggressiveness, and sheer stupidity are all, in their way, psychic diseases that make us unjust, and we do such people no favor at all if we allow them to continue to live in such a state.[13]

If injustice is the suppression of reason and the rule of the lowest human qualities over the highest, then the unjust are no less unfair to themselves than to others. In the normal view, however, this is as Thomas Aquinas put it, merely a "metaphorical" injustice.[14] For does anyone really hurt themselves willingly?[15] If injustice consists of voluntary acts, there must be at least two persons, an agent and a passive victim, and often a third one to decide their conflicting claims. In spite of Aristotelian common sense, however, we are often unjust to ourselves, though not by injuring our souls, as Plato thought. We blame ourselves for acts we did not perform and feel guilty for imaginary faults. We punish ourselves irrationally.

In many older cultural settings, moreover, injustice done to oneself makes a great deal of sense. For the temple robber or murderer, especially the destroyer of his own kin, is polluted, as Plato reminds us. Such a person is also in danger of polluting those near him and of bringing divine wrath upon all. Not only one's community but one's descendants are also endangered, for unexpiated guilt will be inherited by them.[16] The unjust person must be punished and exorcised in order to purify him and the community, and punishment is the only hope of improvement, though it is also meant to teach others to avoid the same crimes.[17] The real roots of the notion that the unjust person is mentally sick are evidently ancient but that does not render it meaningless for less traditional societies. Madness is an extreme case and Plato also reminds us that some acts of injustice, which do not pollute, such as mistreating a slave, will still mar one's own character irremediably. We disfigure ourselves by becoming angry at our inferiors.[18] However, even though the unjust person may be polluted only in extreme cases, he is always self-destructive. And what is required is punishment that will cleanse and cure, even if the cost is life, though exile may also serve the purpose.

Compared to Plato's account of the wretchedness of the unjust person, Aristotle's treatment is undramatic. To be sure, the unjust person does not merely act in a fit of anger or in a moment of passion but does have a permanently warped character as greed becomes habitual. The more often he performs unjust actions, moreover, the worse the whole personality becomes. The dynamic flaw that drives such a person is, however, simple greed, a single fixed trait. Though he took it to be a vice, Aristotle did not mention cowardice and its associated emotions as significant causes of unjust conduct. Yet the fact is that we commit and permit a mass of injustice because we are lazy or afraid or both. Aristotle's unjust agent has only one motive, greed. Moreover, his flaws are to be found wholly in the results of his unfair conduct. We know that he is unjust because he has given too little and taken too much of the desirable and pleasant things that are meant to be shared.[19] The unjust person simply tends to grab whatever is available without concern for anyone else. This is exactly what Aristotle's model of normal justice demands. It can readily succeed in restoring the proper shares to all claimants.

The best fictional characterizations, history, biography, and our own experience tell us that the unjust person has a tangle of many motives, not merely greed. Even if he or she begins with greed and ambition, other dispositions soon come into play. In unjust politics greed is joined by ideology, fanaticism, prejudice, xenophobia, and sexism. Politically there are few more ominous emotional phenomena than the loss of inhibition that collective activity can induce in otherwise decent people.[20] To reduce the impulse to injustice to mere greed is to render most unjust policies virtually incomprehensible.

Not the least of the difficulties of making simple greed the sole motive for injustice is that it seems also to indict the person who takes less than his or her share under the rules, who is not greedy enough. A generous person is not unjust presumably because no one is injured by his or her conduct and one's entire character is improved by such acts.[21] Still, the result of generosity is unjust in two ways. First of all, the consequences are unjust if someone gets less and another more than his or her share, which is what defines injustice. Second, public justice is scorned. For a generous and magnanimous person disdains the pursuit of normal justice and so weakens its political effectiveness. It may indeed be the mark of a noble character to refuse to chase a dollar through the courts but it implicitly lowers the ethical prestige of the juridical order. What matters to the noble person is self-perfection, not the maintenance of a just public order. To be consistent, Aristotle would have had to ascribe limited generosity to the just person to match the uninhibited greed of the unjust. To be sure, perhaps inconsistently, he chose perfection, but many of his heirs settled for moral mediocrity.

All the inadequacies of the moral psychology of the Aristotelian normal model of justice are probably due to the demands of fairness. To be impartial, one may not consider the unjust person as a whole but only those traits and acts that are relevant to decide a given case. Indeed, to look too deeply into the motives of those who take and get too much might lead to unfairness in judging. Greed does well enough as a surface explanation for behavior that really matters to those who must judge. Moreover, it certainly discourages any tendency to sympathize with the lawless. When one thinks of the unjust as Plato did, as victims of a disordered psyche, one may be tempted to pity them rather than those whom they have injured. Although the unjust person is probably not enjoying the good life, the victim is surely worse off, and we should not forget it. Miserable or not, common sense tells us the unjust are not the real victims of their misdeeds. Yet no one seems to find the victims of injustice nearly as interesting as their violators.

The absence of victims is not surprising in the aristocratic ethics of self-perfection. It looks primarily to the character of agents. Neither Plato nor Aristotle paid nearly as much attention to the ultimate victims of injustice as to its perpetrators. It is the unjust citizen-ruler or the tyrants and their distorted souls who matter most. To Plato it seemed that to be ruled by one's political inferiors and to give in to one's lower impulses were parallel experiences of injustice. To live in a disorderly city is bad enough, but to suffer from a self-inflicted indignity, as the unjust person does, is worse. So miserable a creature is a genuine victim. We know that in effect Socrates chose suicide rather than allow himself to suffer such a psychic fate. Only real ignorance could bring one to it.[22]

Even Aristotle, who had a different view—one that precluded any exoneration of unjust persons and which certainly did not regard them as victims—could summon up sympathy for them. No one who really understood what unjust conduct would eventually do to his own character would choose to behave that way. For the result is a personality so diseased that the unjust are worse off than those who are not given their due.[23] Even if we are not encouraged to feel sorry for the unjust person, we are moved to take an interest in his personal situation. We should certainly care enough to arrest his deterioration and to punish him. Christians, of course, are expected to feel compassion for such sinners. They remain conspicuous, far more so than the real victims.

The pursuit of eternal salvation may function just like the aristocratic quest for self-perfection in shunting the victim of injustice aside. In Augustine's *City of God* we are told that the victim of political injustice, the slave in particular, is ultimately less of a victim than the owner because the victim is not exposed to nearly as many temptations. And if she bears her lot patiently, she may expect a better afterlife than her proud master. The slave is in a better position to be spiritually free since she is less shackled to material possessions than the owner is. Again, it is not the socially injured sufferer but the unjust agent who emerges as the real victim.[24] In the sin-ridden world, moreover, it is not only the masters who are victims of their wealth, those who rule are also burdened with special moral dangers. All of the great of this world are doomed. In a Christian view, the powerful are the real victims, while the poorest and most miserable people stand the best chance of avoiding sin. Any picture of the Last Judgment will tell us what an advantage they have.

It is in evident opposition to this grim view and with obvious relish that Nietzsche claimed that in the days of joyful Greek paganism punishments were an entertainment in which one was allowed to vent one's cruelty on the victim.[25] At least there was no doubt in those days who the victim was. Nobody, moreover, worried about the fairness of the proceedings. It does not matter that this is a historical fantasy applicable at most to the gods. It was meant to point to the multiplication of victims and the sanctification of victimhood by the reflective classes of Europe. For Nietzsche it would have been gratifying to believe the average criminal to be a truly assertive man of power rather than a wretched bungler. In fact, most criminals not only fail to be heroic, they may well choose to pretend that they are victims, though as a rule not on Platonic or Augustinian grounds.

Normal criminals will try a number of more obvious dodges, such as arguing that the victims invited attack, especially in rape cases, and entrapped them into crime. They may claim that the complaints are gross exaggerations. In cases of assault or fraud, they are sure to complain that necessity forced them to it. But most significantly for us, they may have learned from Rousseau and his heirs that their acts of injustice were forced upon them by an unjust society that deformed and distorted their moral sensibilities and deprived them of material and moral support, so that again they are the true victims. This should not be taken as mere hypocrisy, but rather as the last in a long line of arguments that treat the criminal as a victim. The force of temptation and the sense of being a constant victim of society are as genuine as all the other arguments that make the unjust person the primary victim of his own conduct or of his surroundings. The Christian view of the injured slave as the beneficiary of the injustice of the master-victim is only a far more extreme example of transforming the unjust person into the true victim. In neither case, however, is the actual victim of an injustice treated as such. The unjust agent is deprived of his self-assertion and the victim's experiences are distorted. The Augustinian and the Nietzschean are both allowed to imagine that it pays to be injured. The victim either goes to heaven or manages to be the victorious oppressor of the truly noble and free individual.

The power of the vicitimized may not be obvious to everyone, but Nietzsche saw their victory as a collective triumph. It was the result of a successful slave revolt led by resentful priests who have always been determined to shackle and destroy the free and noble. It was not an original thought, since Socrates had already been challenged with it by Callicles.[26] Callicles felt victimized and unjustly ruled, not because he was weak and helpless, but because he knew himself to be in every respect superior to most people. He was not getting his due because he could not do as he pleased with them. A mutual-protection society of inferior men had ganged up on him and now governed the city. The feeble had united to fend off their superiors, over whom they now extended their repressive and unjust rule. Far from feeling obliged to knuckle under to the ethical and political system of his tormentors, Callicles had every intention of doing whatever he felt like doing, in spite of their laws and rules.

Callicles is not, one should note, some miserable trickster or petty thief. He is a superb specimen who declares his lawlessness openly because he feels that he has a perfect claim to rule and to rule for his own benefit because he is better than other people in every way. If one accepts his view of himself and of his situation, then he is indeed the victim of the united force of the wretched of the earth. *The Republic* is largely a response to Callicles' defiance, as it is presented by Socrates' agonized young friends, who want him to crush it.

Normal justice has little to say to a Callicles because in the end we are not told that the wisdom of the true rulers, who are his noble opponents, would make them happy. Their lives would be more harmonious and rational if they ruled the city according to a vision of truth rather than as a means to satisfy their interminable and ever-increasing desires, as Callicles would, if he could have it all. Callicles' psychological program is an impossibility, perhaps, but if he is really so superior, there is no reason for him to accept as just the rule of his inferiors, however numerous. He may be a lawless criminal in the making, ripe for ostracism, but from his point of view, he is a victim of a system of conventional justice that does not give him his due as he sees it. From Socrates' point of view, Callicles was also a victim, not of others, but of his own disordered passions. It is a view neither Callicles nor Nietzsche would have shared. It is not how their victims, if they actually had any, would have felt about them either.

What of the real victims of injustice? Philosophy has little to say about them, even when it does not go out of its way to excoriate them. Nevertheless, and in spite of Callicles and Nietzsche, they surely do matter. What about the character of the injured parties? What do we know about them? Unless one takes full account of their experience, the picture of injustice is incomplete. One can see why an aristocratic ethos would be relatively indifferent to them, but no democratic political theory can ignore the sense of injustice that smolders in the psyche of the victim of injustice. If democracy means anything morally, it signifies that the lives of all citizens matter, and that their sense of their rights must prevail. Everyone deserves a hearing at the very least, and the way citizens perceive their social and personal grievances cannot be ignored. The democratic ethos assumes that we all have a sense of injustice and that it plays an important part in the way we judge each other and our society. The voice of the victim, of the person who claims that she has been treated unjustly, cannot therefore, as a matter of democratic principle, be silenced. Who, however, are the victims? What is victimhood like?

It is impossible to characterize victims. They are just people who were in the wrong place at the wrong time in the wrong company. The unjust person has a character, the victim does not even have a role. Many a victim of today will become the victimizer of others tomorrow. Victimhood is a passive notion, as can be seen only too clearly in the very origin of the word *victim*. According to the *Oxford English Dictionary*, victim once referred to living creatures that were killed and sacrificed to some deity. Only since the seventeenth century has it been applied to people who were put to death or subjected to cruel and oppressive treatment. Eventually its meaning was extended to cover those who are merely taken advantage of and even those who suffer as a result of a voluntary undertaking. This definitional expansiveness may well express a growing humaneness but it has hardly reduced the number of human victims among us.

Our abiding cruelty is as evident in the horrors of civil war as it is in the pleasures of laughter. Most of us, moreover, enjoy a good laugh at the expense of victims. Slapstick comedy depends on it. And what is funnier than the innocent bystander who gets a cream pie in his face, slips on a banana peel, and lands in a garbage truck? Social comedy is almost always funny at the expense of hapless victims. Let Molière's immortal *Georges Dandin* stand for all of them. He is a rich peasant who marries into an impoverished noble family. His wife deceives him and his in-laws treat him with contempt and ridicule. And when, halfway through the play he cries out, "I brought it on myself," the audience laughs, and goes on laughing as this poor man's life gets worse and worse. It is far from obvious that we spontaneously side with the injured and rejected. Only some people do, occasionally.

Though it is probably impossible to list all of the forms of victimhood, there is no reason to suppose that purely individual acts of injustice are the cause of all of them. They are certainly conspicuous, but both general human-made and natural disasters are responsible for a great many victims. Indeed, the difference between the two is often crucial for an understanding of injustice. It is, however, not enough to look only at the causes of affliction; the self-understanding of victims must also be taken into account by a full theory of injustice. Moreover, such a theory should concern itself with both *formal* and *informal* victims, both those who are legally or conventionally recognized as such and those who do not show up in even the best of social inventories of injustices.[27] For there are many victims of injustice who fall entirely outside the reach of public rules. This is the case even though democratization has now greatly expanded legal concern for the victims of crime.

Beginning in New Zealand and now in several of the states of the United States, there are laws that provide for compensation, restitution, and social services to victims of crime. Along with these gradual but genuine changes, there is now a flourishing literature on victimology. The horrors of our world since the outbreak of the Second World War and the rise of crimes of violence in American cities have inspired most of it. Its authors tend to be radical, people who have noticed that most of the victims of crime, not just the criminals, are poor people. But in spite of the tendentious literature, there is no reason why middle-class victims of broken promises and fraud should not also be taken into account. What makes victimology politically significant is that it shows that the sense of injustice has evoked a democratic response and that it has not merely festered but has led to new institutions.

In spite of these changes, the normal model of justice continues to have severe difficulties in coming to terms with victims. It limits itself to matching their situation against the rules, which is inadequate as a way of recognizing victims. Victimhood has an irreducibly subjective component that the normal model of justice cannot easily absorb. If I am the victim of disappointed expectations, who is to say that I am or am not justified in holding them? Was there a rule, a custom, or an understanding, as I claim, or was there not? Should there have been one? Am I mistaken, dishonest, or right? Who is to decide? Is the victim, who is at a disadvantage—given that we are always unequal in some way—or the apparent beneficiary of her condition to be trusted? That is not all. When social circumstances or ideological change create new expectations that run counter to all previous assumptions, who is to say what rules, if any, do or do not permit a group to feel victimized? Did they make the rules in the first place? Who did and to whose benefit? If there are rules to decide such conflicts, they are far from settled once a challenge is raised. And in a pluralistic society, with many shifting rules and orders in conflict, it is not possible to formalize them at all. Indeed, we often negotiate settlements, many of them far from just, simply to move on with our various projects, and the victims "have to learn to live with" them. It may well be the best we can do. To raise these questions is not to seek or suggest answers, but only to acknowledge what we already know about ourselves.

Political convenience and ethical disagreement are not the only difficulties in knowing who the genuine victims are. People simply differ enormously about what they feel personally to be unjust.[28] We not only often refuse to recognize victims, but they are also frequently not able or willing to present their grievances. In addition, there must be some element of self-identification; many people whom observers might regard as victims do not recognize themselves as such. The battered wife who will neither call the police nor file a complaint is not alone in failing to be a public victim. There are more subtle reasons than fear and helplessness for refusing to be an overt victim and they are often politically very important, especially for members of ascriptive groups.

Social discrimination against members of ascriptive groups especially is a simple sort of fraud. The victims are falsely accused of faults and failures and then treated accordingly. Yet, surprisingly, many of them do not choose to recognize the injustice of their situation. One extreme response to this sort of injustice is simply "to identify with the aggressor" and abjectly accept his denigrations as truly deserved. Here the injured person hates herself but does not think that she is a victim of injustice, only the recipient of the contempt and disdain that she believes she merits.[29] Far less self-destructive is the preference many women show for self-respect over injustice collecting. Many women who are fully aware of injustices in employment practices and in the salary rates for women in general will nevertheless deny, in spite of evidence to the contrary, that they personally have ever been treated unjustly; there are always a dozen circumstances that make their own cases exceptional and thus not really unjust. Blue-collar workers are known to do the same thing frequently. This may upset people who wonder why they do not behave in the ways Marx thought they should, but it is understandable. Most people hate to think of themselves as victims; after all, nothing could be more degrading. Most of us would rather reorder reality than admit that we are the helpless objects of injustice. Even self-deception is better than having to admit defeat.[30]

There are also ways of turning victimhood to apparently good account and transforming it into an advantage. Even the victims of ascriptive injustice, especially of racial and religious discrimination, may draw pride and strength from comparing themselves to their tormentors, as many Jews have done through the centuries. But, in truth, many more suffer in silence and blame themselves. And many victims learn to be helpless, as women often do, which allows them to evade the conscious status of victimhood but at an awful cost to themselves. Ultimately, a refusal to face up to injustice is neither realistic nor fair. It is merely comforting, for it appears that most of us have a strong need to believe in a just world in which people usually get what they deserve. Blaming the victim is a common response but it is not due only to mean-spiritedness. It also expresses our need to trust the social order in which we live.[31]

Nevertheless, in spite of our usual indifference and worse, it is not the actual and conscious victim only who recognizes injustice for what it is. People who for ideological reasons take up the cause of the victims often have no personal experience of injustice and its humiliations. Politics, especially the politics of protest, is not a selfish enterprise. Conviction, not self-interest, is the driving impulse, especially in symbolic politics. The most radical French Canadian students admitted readily that their personal lives were going very well, and the people who most objected to school busing to achieve racial integration rarely had children in the affected schools.[32] People who take up the political causes of the wretched of the earth often do not have to suffer from a personal sense of injustice.

Those political agents who choose to identify with victims act as they believe the latter should; one might say they become stand-ins for enfeebled victims. They are more likely to engage in political protest. In fact, the people who fight back tend to have a cause and a positive sense of their own worth and powers. They may, of course, also be dangerous fanatics, and we may prefer a measure of injustice to their righteous zeal and the kind of political rule they might impose on us. Nor should we forget the political con men, those who can turn the grievances of others to their own advantage. These are bad citizens, to say the least, but they are not the only ones, although they do remind us of just how dangerous an unremitting sense of injustice can be.

Injustice flourishes not only because the rules of justice are violated daily by actively unjust people. The passive citizens who turn away from actual and potential victims contribute their share to the sum of iniquity. It is one of the failings of the normal model that it looks only to agents, not to the inactive contributors to injustice. It is not a necessary weakness. Indeed, it was a Roman lawyer of distinction, Cicero, who illuminated with great effect the universal prevalence of passive injustice. He was also skeptical in many ways, but unlike Plato he had not given up on republican citizenship. He was, moreover, far less limited in his views than one might suppose from Augustine's assault on him. As a distinguished jurist he was an ardent adherent of the normal model, with a special concern for the fairness and availability of public judicial services. His criticisms were sharp, precisely because he thought that we knew enough to be just. The flaws he did find in the normal model were political, not cognitive. His was thus a civic not a philosophical contribution to the theory of injustice.

Cicero so expanded and embellished the normal model that he gave the idea of injustice a new dimension. When he reflected on injustice he had been driven from public life. In a deep bitterness of spirit, he came to see it in places where most Romans did not choose to look, such as in their treatment of the loyal allies they destroyed when it suited them to do so. He also worried that law itself might, in becoming refined and complex, create its own injustices. But his real originality was in emphasizing two kinds of injustice, one active and the other passive.[33] "Who does not prevent or oppose wrong when he can, is just as guilty of wrong as if he deserted his country." It is a notion that has special importance for any theory of republican citizenship, ancient or modern.

Passive injustice is more than failing to be just, it is to fall below personal standards of citizenship. Clearly, in Cicero's republican ideology injustice acquired a far greater scope than it has in the normal model of justice, which tends to consider only active misconduct. It ignores the ills that we cause by simply letting matters that are not our immediate concern take their course. There is no mention of passively unjust people in Aristotle, though Plato, as one might expect, was well aware of them. He thought that when a young thug beats up an old man, the able-bodied persons who do not interfere are just as guilty as the attacker.[34]

It is important to note that passive injustice is a strictly civic notion. It does not need the support of any particular moral philosophy, utilitarianism, whether negative or positive, contractarianism, or a theory of duty. Any one of these could serve to develop a theory of active republican citizenship that would condemn passive injustice. Purely human moral conflicts are, moreover, not its concern.[35] Passive injustice refers to our public roles and their political context—citizenship in a constitutional democracy. The subjects of terrorist governments, whether modern or traditional, cannot reasonably be expected to behave politically the way citizens of a free republic do.[36] The latter have different rights, responsibilities, possibilities, and expectations of each other. Passive injustice defines the failure of these republican citizens to perform their chief tasks: to see to it that the rules of justice are maintained and to support actively those informal relations upon which a republican order depends and which its ethos prescribes. It should not be enough for them to wait until the agencies of government act when a public wrong has been obviously committed.

To be passively unjust is not to lack charity, which demands more of us. The saintly person offers help that goes beyond human rules and even the call of duty; he is really superior to anything that can be called just or right. The passively unjust man is not accused of failing to go beyond duty, but of not seeing that citizenship involves more than normal justice demands. The normally unjust man is guilty of falling below law and custom by actively violating them and also by being unfair. The passively unjust man, however, does something different; he is simply indifferent to what goes on around him, especially when he sees fraud and violence. His failure is specifically as a citizen. It is not a matter of lacking general human goodness. When he sees an illegal action or a crime, he just looks the other way.[37] If he is a public official his offence is very grave. He is a tyrant who condones injustice by ignoring it or a negligent official who does nothing to mitigate and prevent social and natural disasters. It is he who is always the first to say, "life is unjust" and forget the victims.

In Ciceronian thought injustice is a civic vice unique in character and extent. It is not the sum of all wickedness or total unrighteousness but it does cover all those vices that mark bad governments and the indifferent citizens who allow them to arise and flourish, even though they might have prevented them. As a failing, it is typical of people who enjoy the benefits of constitutional democracy but do nothing to maintain it. The unjust are not only those who benefit directly from unjust acts but those who shut their eyes to the injustice that prevails in their midst.

In our cities, a Ciceronian would see not only the injustices committed by officials, criminals, and cheats but also, emphatically, those of citizens who refuse to report crimes, to notify the police, to give evidence in court, and to come to the aid of victims merely because it is inconvenient. They say nothing about laws and ordinances they regard as unjust and oppressive. If they have any reason to be afraid to act, the burden of guilt falls on their neighbors and the police. But the typically passive citizen is not in that position, he simply would rather let someone else do his duty for him. He is a free rider and little else. Typically, he does not vote, attend meetings, keep informed, or speak up. And it is a judgment on the polity in which the citizen lives, if it encourages him to be passive.

What is the person like who does not stop violence and fraud when he can do so? To be passively unjust is not to fail to rise above one's ordinary civic duty to perform acts of supererogation or to be saintly and heroic, which may not be acts of duty at all.[38] To prevent fraud and violence when we can do so is an act of citizenship, not of humanity. And we are passively unjust not only in sensational cases such as that of Kitty Genovese, who was murdered while her neighbors watched from their windows, too indifferent or scared to call the police, but when we close our eyes to small daily injustices, even for such harmless motives as not wanting to make a fuss, to be a busybody, or to disturb the peace, such as it is.

When we let the wife beater next door go to it rather than interfere, or when we close our eyes to a colleague who routinely grades randomly and arbitrarily out of sheer laziness, we are passively unjust. We may say that family feuds are private matters and that the wife is not likable in any case. We can argue that departmental civility is more important than fairness to students but we would still be paying for peace with injustice. What these examples suggest is that no one has a greater burden of passive injustice to bear than the individual citizen. Our cowardice and evasion have public as well as private consequences. American citizenship, after all, finds its glory not simply in the right to political participation but in the democracy of everyday life, in the habits of equality, and the mutuality of ordinary obligations between citizens. It is an ideal that often fails because we so often choose to be passively unjust.

Take the case of a shopper who is given the wrong change by the cashier in a supermarket. It amounts to $2.50, a considerable amount for him. He protests, but the cashier brushes him off. The cashier is clearly being actively unjust. The woman next to the shopper in line is passively unjust if she does not interfere at this point, and there is really no excuse for her. Her motives may range from misanthropy to merely being in a rush, but that does not alter the fact of avoidance in the absence of any danger to herself. We have reliable empirical evidence to show that if she were alone in the line she might interfere, but if there are several other people around her she will do nothing, partly out of a fear of appearing conspicuous and partly in the hope that someone else will assume the responsibility. Most people in such situations are perfectly aware of what they are doing: they are collaborating with injustice but cannot bring themselves to act, even though they are in the best position to put a halt to the mischief they have observed.[39]

The injured shopper now goes to the store manager to complain. She, however, also brushes him off. It is surely her job to attend to his complaint; we might say that given her role, she is just as actively unjust as the cashier, perhaps even more so. There is a hierarchy here and her responsibility should be as great as her authority to run the store. It should be her business, not the other shopper's, to see that no one gets shortchanged. As a manager as well as a citizen, she is being doubly unjust. She does not see it that way because there is a real labor shortage in Ruritania and she has a duty to keep the atmosphere among the employees reasonably happy. She sees her role as a manager from the inside and regards her duties there as constituting extenuating circumstances. It is, however, not a conflict of roles only that moves her, but ideology. And ideology can never be ignored when one assesses injustice. Our manager is an ardent communitarian; her employer also tends to hire and protect members of their common ethnic and religious group. They have been brought up to believe that to maintain these ties and the traditions that hold their group together have a greater claim upon their loyalties than the rules of society at large. They regard this ethos as one that other groups should adopt as well. Our manager will reprove and correct the cashier later, but not in the presence of strangers. The wrongs done by the employees will thus not be a matter of indifference to her, but justice to an outsider matters far less to her, as a matter of morality, than the bonds of communal solidarity.

Let us say at the very least that the manager of the store has, after all, been hired to run a smooth operation and has an ideologically valid excuse for her conduct. So she sends our shopper to the Ruritanian customer small claims and complaints court. There he is turned away because the court does not take on cases under $5.00. This is in keeping with primary justice because Ruritanians made it clear in the last election that they did not want tax revenues to be spent on extra civil servants to administer services but instead to build new schools and sewage disposal facilities. Education and health are truly important values here. Yet $2.50 is a lot of money for our poor senior citizen shopper, and he certainly has every reason to feel that he has been treated unjustly by everyone. All he got was the bum's rush.

Who was most unjust? The cashier and the silent fellow shopper have no excuse at all, unlike the others. The latter is a pure citizen in this story with no countervailing obligations. She is the most passively unjust. The evasion of the manager must be measured against her responsibilities, but her ideological stance is not a wholly worthless claim. The court had no choice but to act as it did. It was not just obeying orders but behaving as a democratic institution should. As far as these onlookers can see, it is, of course, merely a misfortune. No one is in a position to do anything about the initial injustice of the cashier or to respond to the poor shopper. It all began as an injustice but became a mishap. Tough luck. In fact, all of these people could have stepped outside the rules of their "games" and done something about the man's complaint. They are all passively unjust. The citizen just stood there, the manager preferred community to justice, and even the court clerk could have had a private word with the owner of the shop. There are only two possible conclusions to be drawn from this perfectly common occurrence. We do not care as much about justice as we say and really prefer peace and diversity with injustice, and there is no possible way to reduce injustice significantly without a massive and effective education in civic virtue for each and every citizen. As we prefer liberty to this prospect, it is fair to say that we choose to be passively as well as actively unjust; work hard at inventing plausible excuses for our countless acts of injustice. The most common of these dodges is to redefine injustice as misfortune.

One of the reasons why there is no cure for injustice is that even reasonably upright citizens do not want one. This is not due to disagreements about what is unjust but to an unwillingness to give up the peace and quiet that injustice can and does offer. In this they may well be right. A decent society requires a bundle of positive conditions, among which peace and a general spirit of tolerance are certainly not insignificant. A sophisticated skeptic might thus also favor accepting an amount of passive injustice as a price well worth paying for other social goods. She might also remark that active citizenship does not automatically translate into wise, just, or humane policies. The active citizen may be a good neighbor but he might, just as likely, be a raging bigot or revolutionary, or both.

The recognition of the limits of justice should not be taken as a supine acceptance of all and any forms of injustice. It is difficult to imagine that citizens would choose freely to live under a tyranny, unless they expected to be among its immediate beneficiaries. The peace and quiet that modern dictators promise rarely materializes, as some of their supporters come to know to their cost. There is, however, no denying that tyrants do not lack adherents on whom they can rely. For a truly oppressive government may not only be actively unjust, it may also encourage injustice in its subjects. Though the passively unjust person is first and foremost an ordinary citizen, he is also often a ruler or a public official. Governments that do nothing are often the most unjust of all.

There is, indeed, a perfect representation of such a ruler in the Arena Chapel in Padua, Giotto's *Ingiustizia*.[40] It is in the center of the other vices, replacing the Christian sin of pride, but it is not without religious significance, for it is a male profile that looks to the right at that part of the *Last Judgment*, that depicts in incomparable detail the horrors of hell. The face of Giotto's Injustice is cold and cruel with small, fanglike teeth at the sides of the mouth. He wears a judge's or ruler's cap, but it is turned backward and in his hand is a nasty pruning hook, not a scepter or miter. As he has sown, no doubt so shall he reap, for some of the trees that surround him are rooted in the soil beneath his feet where crime flourishes. Around him is a gate in ruin, but under him we see the real character of passive injustice.[41] There is a theft, a rape, and a murder. Two soldiers watch this scene and do nothing, and neither does the ruler. The woods, always a dangerous place, are unguarded; they are the place where the sort of men who prosper under passive injustice can be as violent as they please. They have a cruel tyrant to govern them, but he and they deserve, indeed engender, each other. The trees around these figures are not "the fruit of the Spirit" but "the work of the flesh," as Paul wrote in his list of sins, and they are not just sown by active injustice but by a government that passively lets it happen.[42] It is

Giotto, *L'Ingiustizia*, Cappella degli Scrovegni, Padua. Courtesy of Alinari/
Art Resource, New York.

a perfect illustration of Justice Brennan's impassioned dissent from from the appalling *DeShaney* decision: "Inaction can be every bit as abusive of power as action, oppression can result when a State undertakes a vital duty and then ignores it."[43]

Unlike some of Giotto's other vices, Injustice does not appear to suffer at all; he seems completely affectless. Envy has a snake coming out of her mouth and recoiling back into her body. Anger is a woman who, in an agony of rage, tears her own chest. Her face is a mirror of pain as all of her dreadful passion is turned against herself. Clearly Giotto had a less sanguine view of anger than Aristotle, who thought that in spite of its pains, anger did have its pleasures since it looked forward to revenge. To fail to show a due anger would be a sign of smallness of soul and a serious character defect.[44] Giotto, however, saw vicious people as tormented people, many of whom were miserable on earth, and all of whom were doomed to eternal punishment. In that sense, his Injustice is also an ultimate victim.

It is no comfort to us, however, to know that Injustice will end in Giotto's hell, as long as we still get raped, robbed, and murdered. What we have learned is what the completely unjust official is really like. He simply does not care at all about what happens to other people as a result of his own or anyone else's conduct. Whether he is charged with governing or is a private citizen, it does not matter to him one way or the other whether other people are injured. The unjust public person is thus revealed as either bold enough to deprive others of their dignity and life or indifferent to it. Though he may be the victim of his own wickedness, he does not arouse our sympathy because we see him as his victims see him. He is, in any case, an impersonation of injustice itself as we all practice it.

The political point is that the unjust citizen, like Injustice himself, is not to be regarded only as violent or greedy but as morally deaf and dissociated. He is responsible for maintaining and serving bad governments and in daily life for allowing fraud and aggression. What he does to the victims of injustice is not only to assault them directly but to ignore their claims. He prefers to see only bad luck where the victims perceive injustice. It is not surprising that they are angry. Aristotle may have believed that anger had its pleasures, but I think that Giotto was closer to the truth. Nothing is more painful or soul-destroying than rage. If we cause rage by arousing a sense of injustice, we cannot measure the harm we do by simply taking the tangible deprivation into account. We must also add the psychological harm we inflict and especially the lasting anger that we inspire. One need only consider the injuries of racial discrimination to recognize that it is not only unjust to deprive people of their social rights but it is also unjust to make them feel the fury and resentment of being humiliated. Nor should we ignore the political costs of organized rage.

Giotto's portrait tells us how injustice looks to the victims, not to some aloof observer. His Injustice is a public menace, a physical threat to all, not only because of what he does but because he is indifferent to the fate of other people and to the impact of his conduct on them. We know him best as the passive beholder of the humiliation of others. In Giotto's picture the moral psychology of injustice is displayed in all its depth. It tells us what the unjust public agent is really like far more completely than the normal model of justice does because it expresses an unattenuated sense of injustice. No theory of either justice or injustice can be complete if it does not take account of the subjective sense of injustice and the sentiments that make us cry out for revenge. Yet the very existence of juridical institutions contributes to our awareness of many of the injustices in our midst. Official justice has a built-in paradox. The better it performs, the greater public consciousness of injustice becomes, and with such awareness come increased demands for effective revenge as well as for more juridical services. It is a political race that judicial institutions can never win.

To the skeptical observer it seems clear that in its cognitive complacency the normal model forgets the irrationality, cupidity, fear, indifference, aggression, and inequality that give injustice its power. The normal model of justice, to which we cling, is not really given to investigating the character of injustice or its victims. It does not tell us everything we should know about either one. Indeed, its very aims prevent it from doing so. The ethical ends of a theory of justice, as of justice itself, limit its intellectual range. Both respond to the requirements of juridical rationality, impersonality, fairness, and impartiality. Probity in this case acts as an inhibition to speculation. That is as it should be. The judicial mind-set looks only at what is relevant to its social aims, not to everything we should know about misfortune and injustice.

The tasks of political theory are, however, quite different and less circumscribed. They can and should raise every possible question about injustice as a personal characteristic, as a relation between individuals, and as a political phenomenon. Above all, political theory cannot turn away from the sense of injustice that is an integral part of our social and personal experiences, whether private or public, and that plays an essential part in democratic theory and practice. It is ideally suited to investigate the question of how to separate injustice from misfortune. Such an inquiry is bound to create puzzles rather than to solve them, but from a skeptical point of view that is no defect.

For instance, do we blame the immediate agent, human or divine, who brought a disaster down upon us? Or should we look to powerful collective causers, perhaps remote in time and place? What is natural and what is human-caused, and does it matter? What could have been averted and mitigated, and who could have seen to it? Why do we either blame irrationally or accept our fate too easily? What is and what is not inevitable or necessary, and how good are excuses offered to victims of disasters who are told: "Life is like that," "nature is unjust"? How much injustice is there? The skeptic will not venture to settle these tormenting problems but, unlike those who look only at justice and its certainties, she means to give injustice its due.

2 MISFORTUNE AND INJUSTICE

The modern age has many birthdays. One of them, my favorite, is the Lisbon earthquake of 1755. What makes it such a memorable disaster is not the destruction of a wealthy and splendid city, nor the death of some ten to fifteen thousand people who perished in its ruins, but the intellectual response it evoked throughout Europe. It was the last time that the ways of God to man were the subject of general public debate and discussed by the finest minds of the day. It was the last significant outcry against divine injustice, which soon after became intellectually irrelevant. Theologians and some lay people, of course, continued to wonder why God allowed the innocent to suffer, but the question was taken off the general intellectual agenda. From that day onward, the responsibility for our suffering rested entirely with us and on an uncaring natural environment, where it has remained.

The citizens of Lisbon were not the only ones to ask, Why were we so afflicted? Voltaire, Rousseau, and Kant were merely the most remarkable voices among many who tried to answer that question. Some sixty years later Goethe would recall how deeply it had disturbed him as a little boy. How could a just and benign God destroy the just and unjust alike? All around him the clergy and the citizens of Frankfurt warned and argued and trembled as the particulars of the disaster became known.[1]

In the shattered city itself few people thought that this was simply a natural event, like annual floods. Many, and especially the clergy, claimed that the earthquake was a just punishment visited by God upon a sinful city. Others, however, while admitting the wickedness of Lisbon's people, did not think they were worse than others. Why us? and Why now? seemed to have no clear answer. As we know, there are no adequate responses to these anguishing perplexities, then or now. But the Jesuit preacher, who all too successfully called upon the populace to pray and repent, was put to death by the Marquis de Pombal, who was in charge of restoring order to Lisbon and who had to see to it that the city be made livable again. There was no time for penances and prayers. Pombal's orders were, moreover, buttressed by a widely shared belief that though God was just, he was utterly incomprehensible.[2]

While the people of Lisbon tried to pick up their lives, the rest of Europe took to speculation. The first blast came from Voltaire. He had long been repelled by Pope's and Leibnitz's cosmic optimism with its "whatever is, is right" or at least necessary for some universal good. *Poem upon the Lisbon Disaster* is a sustained assault upon the trite axiom, "all is well."

Seeing these stacks of victims, will you state,
Vengeance is God's, they have deserved their fate?

What is God doing to us? Surely there is no need for this!

He is unshackled, tractable, and just.
How comes He, then, to violate our trust?

The book of fate is closed to us, evil is palpably everywhere, and while God may exist, he will certainly not help humanity. Voltaire advises us to play it safe, like his hero, Candide. But the sense of betrayal, which is the very core of the sense of injustice, has not been quieted. It seethes in every line of the poem.[3]

Voltaire's quarrel with God was bound to inflame Rousseau,

since it seemed to divert attention from the real perpetrators of injustice, the rich and powerful. Ever the man of the people, Rousseau fired off a blast reminding Voltaire that he was depriving the poor and miserable of their last and only hope, their faith in a kind deity and an afterlife. The earthquake was a natural event; it was a disaster only because people had built houses six or seven stories high. In a desert or a village of huts it would have caused no injuries. It is our own fault. The clergy and the philosophers were equally wrong to drag Providence into natural events. The former were superstitious while the latter were so vain that they blamed Providence when they had a toothache. What was needed was a new civil religion that would satisfy both the spiritual and the social needs of ordinary people, not a disheartening anti-theology fit only for the idle and bored.[4] The poor and rejected had enough misery to bear and did not need the burden of cosmic despair as well.

Yet the two were not as far as apart as Rousseau tried to pretend. "Sinister accidents" were not an alien thought to him either. In his *Discourse on Inequality*, he had claimed that some such cataclysm must have driven us out of our natural contentment into an artificial and always-damaging social existence. He was far from denying the presence of evil; no one saw it more clearly. He merely did not want to blame God for what was our doing. In effect, he banished God from our lives far more completely than Voltaire had. Indeed, we do not even know exactly how our greatest disaster occurred. But however it began, no worse disaster had or has ever befallen us than our departure from nature to culture. What greater cosmic injustice can be imagined than an accident that dooms us to insuperable inequality and oppression?[5] It was in order to concentrate on this, our real, social misfortune, that Rousseau scornfully rejected Voltaire's metaphysical protest.

Kant was still a young lecturer on scientific subjects at the time of the Lisbon disaster. In the three essays he devoted to earthquakes after hearing about it, he was, not surprisingly, very close to Rousseau's ideas. He offered his readers an account of the prevailing scientific explanations of earthquakes, assured them that they were necessary and in some respects even beneficial, and finally warned them not to scrutinize the ways of God that could never be known. Nor should they waste time trying to invent superhuman technologies. If people want to do something about the real misfortunes that destroy humankind, they should end war—by far the most devastating of all disasters.[6] It was a point that Cicero had already made when he also compared natural and human-made disasters.[7] It is not a thought that anyone is likely to miss at present, but it is not new, which should not surprise us when we recall the fate of Carthage and that Germany in 1648 looked much the way it did in 1945.

Even as they enhanced God's powers by stressing his creation and control over endless planets, the philosophers removed him from the immediate concerns of humanity, such as the Lisbon earthquake. Neither the suffering of individuals, nor the disasters in which large numbers of people perish are of the slightest interest to him. The phrase "act of God" has become a cynical excuse for avoiding legal liabilities. Only random bad luck and necessity remain to relieve us of responsibility. Nevertheless, irrationally and inconsistently to be sure, we continue to accuse life of being unfair and nature of being unjust. In fact, we often blame ourselves wholly without grounds, simply because an arbitrary and wholly impersonal world seems harder to endure than an unjust one in which some force, at the very least, is in charge of events.

WHO IS TO BLAME?

Someone simply must be blamed to maintain the unquenchable belief in a rational world, but the exculpation of God has not made it easier to know whom to accuse. Nor has it helped us to decide which of our travails are due to injustice and which are misfortunes. When can we blame others and when is our pain a matter of natural necessity or just bad luck? As we have seen already, it is always difficult to distinguish genuine victims from false claimants. Because we are all potentially both victims and victimizers, we can readily see an accident or a disaster from either perspective. If we identify with the victim, we are likely to cry injustice, but we will see misfortune if we think that we might be the actual or even imaginable victimizer. There seems to be no measuring rod at all. If the proverbial neutral observer were to decide that on the evidence available there was no answer to the question, Who did this to the poor sufferer? and told the victim to resign himself, he might be wrong in his conclusions. The victim may well continue to feel injured, and his social expectations may still be deeply disappointed by an obvious public indifference to the consequences of the disaster just suffered. At this point his sense of injustice has been aroused by passive, not active, injustice, by failures to prevent or mitigate his present condition. Our readiness to act is implicated here, as it so often is when we have to decide whether injustice has or has not been done. And there is always a strong impulse to do nothing, if at all possible. We all tend to be passively unjust.

The very distinction between injustice and misfortune can sometimes be mischievous. It often encourages us to do either too much or too little. That something is the work of nature or of an invisible social hand does not absolve us from the responsibility to repair the damage and to prevent its recurrence as much as possible. Nor can we respond to every unjust act. America's favorite game, passing the blame, is not always constructive. The search for human perpetrators may actually have only limited use, as a prelude to extracting compensation for victims or as a possible deterrent to future recklessness. On the border between misfortune and injustice we must deal with the victim as best we can, without asking on which side her case falls.

It is, however, a rationalist fantasy to imagine that we will ever give up looking for injustice or accepting misfortune as an excuse. It is not even to be wished for. Our sense of injustice is our best protection against oppression. Let no one lull us into forgetting Voltaire's unyielding protest. We also need to remember that there really are misfortunes to which we must resign ourselves, lest we fall into fantasies of omnipotence and total safety. The notion of misfortune refers to the fact that there are limits to what we can accomplish, especially by technological means, for which we instantly reach in our dreams of mastery. They tend only to encourage us to avoid hard choices.

The contrast between misfortune and injustice should survive, not only for psychological and political reasons. In a democracy we are supposed to castigate public agents who do nothing about disasters and accidents—either to prevent them or to lighten their consequences. They are, in their indolence and indifference, passively unjust. Indeed, we ought to direct our sense of injustice less toward the search for possible initiators and the immediate causes of disasters than toward those who do nothing to prevent them or to help the victims. Civil servants in a democracy are supposed to be responsible to the public. Our first suspicions should be turned toward governmental and semipublic agencies because it is not unlikely that they could have done more in the past and should do more in the future to ensure our safety. Even though the disastrous burdens left us by our deceased predecessors or the work of the invisible hand and a harsh but predictable nature cannot be identified as actively unjust, they are amenable to improvement. Those who can alter their course or avert their effects are passively unjust if they do nothing at all. In politics, the difference between misfortune and injustice clearly makes sense and can serve our interests—if we use it intelligently.

In any case, our sense of injustice, no less than our apparently inexhaustible and profound need to discern some purpose in the natural world, will ensure that we will go on to blame and to curse when unmerited pain comes to us. We have no less a psychologist than William James's word for it that we experience an earthquake as a personal offense, an evil act directed at us. He happened to be in Palo Alto at the time of the great San Francisco earthquake; this is what he wrote about it: "I personified the earthquake as a permanent individual entity. . . . It came directly at *me*. It stole in behind my back and, once inside the room, had me all to itself, and could manifest itself convincingly. Animus and intent were never more present in any human action, nor did any human activity ever more definitely point back to a living agent as its source and origin." And, "For me *the* earthquake was the *cause* of the disturbance and the perception of it as a living agent was irresistible. It had an overpowering dramatic convincingness."[8] He thought it natural that "untutored men" should see warning and retribution in such an event. If that is how William James felt, it is hardly surprising that the rest of us also feel that we are being singled out for attack and respond accordingly by looking for someone to blame. The more unexpected and unendurable the fear and suffering, as when we lose a child to a painful death, the more we feel that we have been singled out unjustly. The question, Why me? or Why us? cries out for something other than an explanation; it calls for something that makes moral sense.

Thus, physicians have observed a pattern of responses to grief in which the sense of injustice, of having been betrayed, has a normal place. The first reaction is disbelief, then questioning: Why did this happen and how? and then comes anger, Why him (or her)? "I can think of a lot of people who deserved this more than she (or he)." And "you can't love God." This is followed by resignation and ultimately by resolution. Some patients, before they can accept the fact of a life-threatening disease, will bargain with God. Significantly, even people without any religious faith at all will curse God when they are told that their child must die. When some event completely disrupts our private or social equilibrium, we demand at the very least justification from God. Even self-blame, guilt, and shame are preferable answers to "Why me?" than total silence or a mindless moral vacuum.[9]

Only one group of people like to see flukes or pure accidents and are eager to claim that disasters are "just one of those things." They are those who fear that they may be potentially or actually implicated or blameworthy. For them it is a self-protecting move, with a view to similar future events. Typically, they have no reason to think of themselves as victims or as related to them.[10] They look for rational explanations as a rule. But for the afflicted there must be more than that, something more personal, like an injustice, not merely a random disappointment.

As one looks at the historical record of self-accusations,

scapegoatings, manipulations of supernatural forces, and searches for conspiracies, one may conclude that we may well have a far greater need to believe in the prevalence of injustice than to see things as they really are. While we cling to a belief in a just world as long as we can, even an unjust universe is more tolerable than a senseless one. We often seem to blame ourselves and each other in order to establish a coherent story about causes and events, not as a preparation for action. Not that choosing to accept misfortune is always realistic. Far from it. It may simply imply an unreasoning fatalism. Sometimes, of course, we may really be paralyzed by an inability to decide whether an event or state of affairs should be regarded as a misfortune, an injustice, or a bit of both. But it is a puzzle in which our preferences, status, perspective, and political ideology are all implicated, especially when public policy may be at stake.

Is it, for example, a misfortune or an injustice to be a woman? What about famines? unemployment? poverty? To a great extent, our answer to such conundrums will depend on what we know or choose to believe to be inevitable and unalterable. And political ideology has much to contribute to our sense of necessity. It does not follow that a powerful sense of injustice will always incline us to see avoidable human conduct and wrongdoing in all disasters, but it will move us, as it moved Kant, to come down hard on those causes of human misery for which we are undeniably and solely responsible, like war. One is bound to suspect that a too-ready acceptance of the social necessity of many disasters may be ideologically convenient rather than an iron law of historical or economic development. Surely human prayers, curses, and justifications in the face of accidents and disasters testify to our refusal to resign ourselves to an endlessly cruel world.

Polytheism blames its many gods, Manichaeans may yield to despair, while the monotheist trembles before a vengeful god. All at least know why it is happening.[11] Jews tend to blame themselves, personally or collectively. Job's friends are perfectly representative men when they remind him of God's justice and the innumerable flaws of men. "Who ever perished being innocent?" and "Does God pervert justice?" they ask the long-suffering Job.

Passivity clearly recommends itself before such a deity. Manipulation of supernatural powers is, however, more normal. Elaborate magical rites to end epidemics are common. In medieval Europe the flagellants and wild dancers were trying only to exorcise the evil spirits that were causing the Black Death. In the absence of alternative beliefs, the lack of success does not appear to discourage these ritual responses.[12] A fatalistic "it just happens" attitude is what is really uncommon.

Deities are not the only powerful forces that get blamed, especially now. Today, even fundamentalist Christians in America do not blame God for disasters. Some do lose their faith in God and nature in a "you wonder about his doings" response, but most know whom to blame and from whom to get relief, and it is not God.[13] They blame the local companies and public authorities and look to the federal government for disaster relief. Billy Graham was an exception among evangelical preachers when he claimed that the Waco, Texas, tornado of 1953 showed "what God can do if we do not repent."[14] Most Americans take the forces of nature as something to be mastered and repaired, in keeping with their understanding of technological potential, though there are cultural variations in the level of passivity among various ethnic groups.[15] Individuals obviously also meet personal disasters in different ways, depending on their psychological makeup. Some terminal patients blame an unjust fate. "The good always suffer," they say, and resign themselves to an unjust world. Others do nothing of the sort.

For an understanding of injustice, it is those victims who feel guilty who are the most significant, for they are clearly unjust to themselves. One danger is that they may be so ashamed that they will not seek medical help in time.[16] It is one of the meaner aspects of our superstitious culture that having cancer is thought to be a disgrace, like losing one's job, which is also blamed on the victim. The sick and fired are not alone in their feelings of guilt. Mere survival can make those who were part of a great public disaster feel guilty for the rest of their lives. For the question "Why me?" afflicts the survivor as well.

Nevertheless, in spite of its manifest injustice, guilt has its uses.

Patients who blame themselves or others for past sexual offenses are more optimistic than fatalists. That also explains why some victims of destructive natural disasters often return to their homes sooner than is safe, because they feel that they have paid off their guilty deeds and are now immune to further troubles. They are in a healthy hurry to restructure their lives. Guilt also allows one to bargain. Soldiers going into battle often abstain from sex in the hope that virtue will be rewarded. Above all, guilt allows one to maintain "the illusion of centrality," the notion that one was singled out, that the emotions that Williams James described make sense, and that each one of us is more than just another statistic.[17] In short, blaming oneself, though unjust, has its satisfactions. It can sustain belief in a just world and give one a sense of at least some power in determining one's situation. To be sure, its costs are not negligible either, because it usually only adds another burden to our fears and sorrows.

Next to guilt, the most truly unjust and unwarranted response to accidents and disasters is scapegoating, especially in serious failures and disasters. Few people can bear the lesson of Cleopatra's nose. They need causes that are as weighty as the result. If there is dreadful human-caused damage, a lot of people, probably important and powerful persons, must be at fault. One need only recall that most spectacular and studied case, the Cocoanut Grove fire on November 28, 1942, in Boston, in which almost five hundred people perished in a nightclub.[18] The immediate cause of the fire was a match dropped into an artificial plant by a teenage busboy. The *real* cause, it was eventually found, was a chemical in the leatherette covering of the seats, which gave off asphyxiating fumes in the fire. Panic and suffocation killed most of the victims. This leatherette covered the benches of most American nightclubs, but too many of the exits were certainly locked that night in the Cocoanut Grove. There were also a number of safety violations, but none was very serious and there was no evidence of bribery to evade inspections. Nothing about the Cocoanut Grove was unusual, given the way business was and is done in Boston.

As usual in sensational disasters of this sort the press was especially intent upon finding a guilty party, more so, in fact, than the friends of the victims, or the survivors.[19] And so for over a month, in the middle of the war, more than 50 percent of Boston's news was devoted to the fire, its investigation, and the indictments that followed. The owner, Welansky, was in due course sent to jail for manslaughter and pardoned only just before his death. As soon as the fire department began its hearings, the *Christian Science Monitor* intoned, "the process of whitewashing is sickening." The actual cause and the moral cause simply had to be separated. The latter could rest only with the fire and police departments, the mayor, and with the entire city government —all in cahoots with the Jewish owner of the Cocoanut Grove. "They" were a mass of corruption and "they" had conspired to bring about the fire, if not directly, in effect.

Then as now, Boston politics was not pure, but there was not a shred of evidence that Mayor Tobin or Welansky were engaged in a cover-up. But what was needed, given the magnitude of the disaster, was a comparable degree of malignity. Day after day, the newspaper found it among "them." Neither the busboy, the locked exits, the fumes, nor the panic would do. Someone important had to bear the blame for palpable wrongdoing. This is not unusual. Both the severity of the losses and the social positions of actual or potential perpetrators determine the amount of blame that will be ascribed in any serious human-error accident, especially in industry or transportation. In Boston, it was the entire political establishment and the owner of the club. And the papers and their readers were sure that this was the case the day after the fire.

All the complexities of disaster caused by "many hands" come together in the Cocoanut Grove fire. The citizens of Boston had every reason to fault the performance of the city government, especially the inspectors. There clearly was laxity and Boston was chronically ill-governed. The calamity, however, was so infinitely greater than any of the immediate or distant misdeeds that had brought it about, that some visible person or group—guilty of deep corruption, criminal greed, and carelessness—had to be found to serve as an adequately blameworthy agent. There had to be a conspiracy and a villain; nothing less would do. The responsibility for the fire was diffuse, and it was absurd to accuse Mayor Tobin of being in league with the owner of the Cocoanut Grove or to accuse the latter of being a willful criminal. As the head of Boston's government, the mayor was certainly responsible for the city's inefficient services, but precisely because the charges were either too specific or too general, they were both unjust and futile. Welansky did not deserve to go to jail, and you get nowhere by blaming the entire establishment.

We blame ourselves and each other unjustly simply to avoid Voltaire's conclusion that the world is a mass of random evil, of bad luck. Even impersonal, shared, tangled responsibility without a face is too much to bear. Like self-blame, conspiracy hunting and scapegoating are anything but fatalistic. Behind every disaster there must be ill-will and fault, and their consequences do not just happen. They are designed to occur, by ourselves and powerful others. Injustice makes sense, and we can cope with it and carry on. For all their variety through the ages, most cultures have encouraged these terrible fantasies because they are often highly functional and do much to maintain social order. In African tribal societies, where there is no technology and much mutual dependence, personal misfortunes are usually blamed on individuals known to the afflicted person. The experience of relying on others for good and ill is simply extended to cover all the things that seem just to happen to us.

Witchcraft is as good an answer to "Why me?" as any. An African teacher told an anthropologist that he understood perfectly well that an infection had killed one of his pupils, but not why that child rather than any of the others who had been exposed to the disease. Witchcraft supplied him with a perfectly acceptable answer.[20] It clearly integrates misfortune into an existing social and moral framework and warns people against giving way to malice. Functional as it may be, it is wholly unacceptable to a modern democratic society, as is the belief of patriarchal societies that the sins of the fathers must be visited upon their children. This is not scapegoating in the modern sense, however, because there is no search for guilty parties, but a shared knowledge about misfortunes that both the victims and their enemies fully accept.

It would also be false to speak of scapegoating in the distribution of blame for failure in the few remaining genuinely hierarchical organizations, such as the United States military. In such social hierarchies, the people at the bottom are expected to obey, but also to trust, their superiors. When the U.S. military fails, those in command must assume the entire burden of responsibility. In addition, all those who depend upon the military to defend them are bound to feel betrayed when they blunder, for American citizens have been encouraged to have great confidence in them. Although the violation of expectations must be fairly conspicuous before blame is ascribed to those who are supposed to protect them, when the disaster is as spectacular as Pearl Harbor, the man in charge must bear all of the public's ire. In fact, it was a result of a complex operational failure and not of Admiral Kimmel's incompetence; but as the man in command, he took most of the censure. To be sure, America is not so unjust a society as to scapegoat him with a charge of treason, but he bore more than his share of the blame because that is how a hierarchy must work if it is to last.

In the military, responsibility has to be personalized at the highest level of the organization since its system of command is built on the principles of obedience and reliance. Military historians may note ruefully that is not how things are done in the corporate world. No one pinned the blame for the Edsel on Henry Ford, but we do not need to rely on our car manufacturers in the way we do have to depend on the military. We cannot afford to be philosophically discriminating when our security depends on maintaining the principles of hierarchical responsibility for victory and defeat, especially the latter.[21] Moreover, if there had been as serious an industrial disaster at one of the Ford plants, the head of the company would have been blamed. So we divorce cause from responsibility because we regard guilt at the top as a

necessary myth. In this we may, of course, be mistaken and looking for trouble because we might end by hiding the historical and
organizational facts from ourselves, which is a very dangerous
thing to do.

In a technologically advanced society, it may well be that a
sense of injustice cannot be as easily satisfied as in traditional
societies. Like revenge, the principle of hierarchical responsibility may be deeply satisfying, but it may be just as incompatible
with the actual workings of a complex modern social order and
may also have to be abandoned as simply too irrational. That
would leave us with a choice of resorting either to scapegoating
or to living with a no-fault response to military disasters.[22]

The choice between punitive blaming and indifference can be
made less drastic if we do not look for personal betrayal of trust,
conspiracy, or culpable incompetence and concentrate more on
failures to prevent avoidable mistakes with a view to making their
recurrence less likely and repairing the damage as well as possible. This is in fact what we already do in many cases. Since, however, we often do not choose to pay the cost of preventing all
avoidable disasters, we can think of ourselves as victims of technological necessity and take out insurance policies to deal with
the consequences. These sensible utilitarian suggestions are not,
however, satisfactory responses to the people whose injuries have
aroused their sense of injustice. They will continue to look for
someone to blame, and it will probably be the government.

To be sure, some fires, floods, storms, and earthquakes are
still recognized as natural and unavoidable, but the government
is expected to warn, protect, and relieve us when they occur. We
no longer have childhood diseases and there are so few epidemics that when one does occur—like AIDS—we are aghast and
victims blame the government for not being able to stop it. What
is perceived in all these cases is that with the technical resources
at our command, we should be able to turn all natural disasters
into manageable setbacks. Our sense of injustice is deeply aroused
when we fail. Our technological expectations are often too high,
but given what the last two generations have accomplished, we

suspect wrongful indifference or injustice when there is no one to protect us against the still-untamed forces of nature. In fact, it is not the fault of scientists or public officials that little can now be done, nor are they culpably indifferent to the current epidemic. Victims, however, seem to find it easier to bear their misfortune if they can see injustice as well as bad luck.

The impulse to blame the government, though often grossly unfair and irrational, is nevertheless not in itself irrational. Injustice is, properly speaking, a social offense of the powerful, and we should make sure that they have not wronged us. Moreover, politics is the sphere of choice and projects; public agents should not be encouraged to feel that they are in the grip of necessity and personally powerless. They can usually perform better and more responsibly than they do and at the very least be guilty of only passive injustice.

WHEN DOES MISFORTUNE BECOME INJUSTICE?

Is there, then, for us in the United States still anything that is not an injustice but a misfortune? What about being a woman? No natural conditions are more subject to social definition than gender and reproduction. Orthodox Jews thank God every morning in their prayers for not having made them women. They are only being honest; it is what most men think. Our entire literature is full of pity for a sex that does not even recognize its own misfortune and must be treated with condescension and occasional abuse. What is the nature of the misfortune? It is located in women's bodies and the part they play in the propagation of the species. Nothing unjust about that. It is just a painful natural necessity, enhanced by many a male imagination that sees women as forces of nature and peculiarly close to the primal sources of life. The sense of fate that is in store for such a being can be found in Thomas Hardy's *Tess of the D'Urbervilles*. Hardy makes it plain that hers is more than a social disaster. She is, as the novel's subtitle has it, "a pure woman," that is, nothing but a woman. That is all she is, and it is explicitly a natural curse. One man seduces her and their child dies. A second man marries her and rejects her when he learns of her past. When the seducer repeats his act she kills him, because she has no other resource for self-assertion. She is then duly hanged for the crime. The story, even without its coincidences and poor characterization, would not be credible. Its force rests on Tess alone; she is all sex, which is what being a pure, natural woman adds up to. The rest follows neces-sarily, like a mythic anathema. It cannot be called unjust, since the novel assumes that Tess was being treated in a legally normal way. The men are bad luck, but her real tragedy is in the structure of nature; it is her femininity. Nothing could give one a better sense of sheer misfortune of being an attractive woman when her life is seen as a conflict between nature and culture.

What if the fate of women were perceived less fatalistically? What if women's disabilities were all rooted in their reproductive functions, from which all other misfortunes follow, and what if there are now technologically feasible means of removing these impediments? Then it is merely an injustice if nothing is done to make these instruments of liberation available to women. Once an expectation of change for the better has been created by a possible way out of a natural misfortune, it becomes unjust to disappoint the hopes of the victims. Their sense of injustice will be aroused and rightly so. If we read Shulamith Firestone we will know exactly who is bilking us out of our freedom. Childbearing can be done artificially and parenting left to those people who want to do it and who are especially qualified for this most demanding of tasks. From that point of view, being a woman was indeed a misfortune once upon a time and is now an injustice. Whether one believes, as Firestone does, that this liberation is historically inevitable or is less sanguine, it is a challenge to our sense of injustice. For to deny women the technical means of liberation is to refuse them something that they have been led to expect, the availability of technologies that free Americans from physical pain and drudgery and permit them to lead full and productive social lives.[23]

One might, of course, suspect that this technological scenario is inadequate, and that it offers neither an explanation nor a full solution to the misfortune of being a woman. Technology has only cast a sharp light on the situation. What if being a woman is not only a physical misfortune but also culturally so ingrained that nothing less than a total transformation of society—nothing short of universal fraternity—can ever mitigate it? Simone de Beauvoir has not denied that being a woman has always been an injustice but sees it as rooted in such a tangled mix of physical and social conditions that it is too deep to be remedied by simple technological opportunities. Moreover, it appears to her that one cannot be just in an unjust society. Being a fortunate exception to the rule, by marrying well and having a decent job, does not alter the conditions of injustice in which one lives as a woman, as a member of a physically and culturally defined group of inferiors. It is more or less like "passing" for white or gentile.[24]

What she does ignore is the possibility of democratic political and social change to lift the injustices endured by women gradually. That still leaves the misfortune. Will it really be one if the injustice ends? Surely it is only a misfortune if we accept it as such and lie down supinely before it. Might my granddaughter not thank God in her prayers that he did not make her a man? Why not? For there is in Beauvoir's own existentialist vision a third possibility, to accept and transform the given by making it one's own project, rather than merely enduring it as an alien imposition.[25] Instead of allowing oneself to submit to the characterization of others, one picks it up, makes the gender differences a point of personal pride, and forges ahead by whatever means are available to assert the freedom and equality of women as women. We are all the work of both nature and history, after all, but we need not remain its passive victims. We all can make an effort to turn misfortune around, see it as injustice, and act on that recognition.

Being a woman is a misfortune that has become an injustice because we want to change our estate. Famines are also not what they used to be and for similar reasons. Like many no-longer pure misfortunes, the immediate onset of famine is caused by natural misfortune but its persistence owes far more to human injustice or folly or both. Because there is a nonhuman element in famines, it is particularly easy to think of them as inevitable, like earthquakes. Even more interesting are the necessities that are invoked by those who choose not to do anything much about them. Indeed, famines throw a harsh light upon the whole notion of necessity in the affairs of human beings.

Consider the famine that lives on in the ancestral memory of many Americans, the Great Hunger in Ireland in the middle of the last century. It began when a fungus destroyed the potato crop. The cause of the blight was not understood and could not have been prevented or halted. Agricultural science was still in its infancy. There was no purely technological answer available. Was it, however, purely a misfortune that so many Irish peasants lived off a single crop, and that the land laws imposed rigid obstacles to agricultural improvement? That might raise the impossible question of historical injustice, but in this case there is every reason to recognize passive injustice. It is not only in retrospect that one sees many alternative policies that the government might have pursued. Many of its contemporary English critics spoke out in favor of change and offered suggestions for a variety of positive and plausible courses of action. The immense contempt that most Englishmen felt for the Irish is also not to be ignored.

Once the famine became truly serious, the problems of alleviation had to be confronted. Many public men felt torn between religion and economic necessity. Religious duty demanded that governments relieve the victims of famine; economic doctrine forbade any interference with free enterprise. The men in charge did just what one would expect. They worked like demons on schemes and reports. No one could charge them personally with callousness or indifference. They discharged their religious duty by ample medical relief, aid to hospitals, and appeals for private charity. But as soon as the Whigs came to power, there was an end to the government depots that Robert Peel had set up to distribute cheap corn to keep food prices down. Nothing was done about the Irish landlords. Indeed, a few choice quotes from statesmen and public servants in London illustrate the hold of the idea of economic necessity on their minds. Thus Cornewall Lewis wrote in a report commissioned by the government that "the scheme of the government managing everything for the people . . . invariably ends by producing lethargy and helplessness in the people." That the Irish were already numb with hunger did not seem to count. What did concern him was that fraud, bureaucratic imcompetence, and disaster would result if capitalists were replaced by governmental agents. The man in charge of the treasury, Charles Trevelyan, noted that "for the government to undertake by its own direct agency the detailed drainage and improvement of the whole country, is a task for which the nature and function of government are totally unsuited." The famine might best be regarded as a solution to the overpopulation that was Ireland's real curse. So in 1846 he wrote, "This [problem] being altogether beyond the power of man, the curse being applied by the direct stroke of an all-wise Providence [was] in a manner as unexpected [and] as unthought of as it is likely to be effectual."

A year earlier Trevelyan had insisted that "there is only one way in which the relief of the destitute ever has been, or ever will be, conducted consistently with the general welfare, and that is by making it a local charge." Since the Irish landlords were as broke as their tenants by then, the imposition of poor-law taxes was a model of realism only in Trevelyan's laissez-faire mind.

The system of landholding was treated as sacred. In Lord Brougham's words, "property would be valueless and capital would no longer be invested in the cultivation of land if it were not acknowledged that it was the landlord's undoubted, indefeasible and most sacred right to deal with his property as he list." Under no circumstances was the "the ordinary course of trade" to be disturbed by the government.[26] There were also political "necessities." Lord John Russell's government would not have survived the reception that any bill limiting the power of landlords would have received in the House of Lords.

The Irish peasantry, generally deeply devout, tended to look upon their suffering as a divine visitation and punishment. Their descendants do not see it that way and, more significantly, neither did many people in England and Ireland at the time of the famine. From the victims' perspective, this was passive injustice, a failure to mitigate suffering that could have been alleviated. Had the victim's voice been treated as the privileged and primary one and had the most activist of the policies that were reasonably proposed been followed, there would still have been plenty of hunger, but no injustice. Neither was possible given the scorn and blame the English heaped upon the Irish victims and the intellectual self-assurance of their economic orthodoxy.

For Trevelyan it was a matter of tragic choice. An evangelical Christian, he felt torn between having to betray his faith or his public duty. For the victims it meant misery and death either at home or on a ghastly voyage to America, especially when disease was added to starvation. This was not a tragic fate at all, and we are right to call it utterly unjust because we know that this sort of conduct was avoidable, inexcusable, and that it should not be repeated. Yet we can do that without looking upon Trevelyan and his like as criminally responsible for their limitations. These men really were a misfortune, since nothing can ever be done about the conventionality of most people, especially officials. Nevertheless, a famine is a politically avoidable disaster. When nothing is done to end one when it begins, there is injustice.

THE POLITICS OF NECESSITY

The Great Hunger is as good an example as any of the uses of ideology in treating passive injustice as misfortune by imposing a sense of tragic inevitability upon events that are in fact entirely amenable to purposive human alteration. In a truly tragic situation there are no good choices, none.[27] It is so overdetermined that human agents must be seen as puppets. Nevertheless, because they are human, they remain responsible for their character and manner of conduct. The tragic world is in the hands of gods who play with us as they choose, often wantonly, though we are still in command of some of our actions. Aeschylus's Agamemnon has no good choice, if it can be called a choice at all. He must either sacrifice his daughter to placate Artemis or disobey Zeus and let his army starve in their ships, unable to set sail without a wind. The chorus does not blame him for killing Iphigenia, but they do reproach him for the way he does it. He distances himself from her as if she were not his child but just another sacrificial animal.[28] Indeed, the perception of unfitness is an integral part of the sense of injustice, even in far less extreme situations than Agamemnon's. When the powerful do not behave as one might expect them to in a disaster, there is added resentment. Some of the survivors of the celebrated Buffalo Creek mine disaster were particularly bitter that the company had made no personal gestures of sympathy to any of them. Similarly, some of the survivors of Hiroshima, although they might accept their fate as part of war, resented President Truman's refusal to express regret for what had been done.[29] Even where there is no choice, the manner of our behavior can render it more or less unjust. Even tragic choices have a better or worse face that expresses the true character of the agent.

Real tragedy is very rare in any case. What is called political necessity is not really fate or a determined situation or tragic in the full sense. Since Machiavelli *necessity* has served to paper over the tension between ethical restraint and political ambition in an effort to exploit the language of doom for the exculpation of rulers. The modern career of this chicanery has certainly been spectacular. Those who have from the first had doubts about Machiavellian "reason of state" thinking, have also found the necessities invoked by princes less than compelling. Montaigne did not think that a man of honor should break his faith for his prince. "The public weal requires men to betray, to lie, and to massacre; let us resign that charge to men who are more obedient and compliant." Clearly honor is either more important than the public weal, or those who rule have a false notion of what the latter is. "If perfidy can ever be excusable, it is only so when it is employed to punish or betray perfidy," Montaigne goes on to say. For him, the conflict is clearly between personal honor and public betrayal. A gentleman can choose the former, but a prince might not always be able to do so. When, therefore, in those extreme and unambiguous cases, when a ruler must act dishonorably, how he does so and in what spirit makes all the difference. "When by urgent circumstances, or some sudden and unexpected event, a ruler is obliged, for reason of state necessity, to shuffle out of his word and break his faith . . . he must regard it as a stroke of the divine rod. . . . It is indeed a misfortune." Such a stain upon one's conscience is worth it only if the public interest is "both very apparent and very important." And it may even be that his honor and good faith should be more important to a prince than his own safety and that of his people.[30]

For Machiavelli, at whom these lines were aimed, the conflict was not between honor and necessity but between moral scruples and politics. His political necessity was imposed not by fate or even by the public weal but by the difficulties of maintaining and expanding a prince's power in a competitive political world. A prince's task is not rendered any easier by the malice and capriciousness of fortune, the goddess who thwarts us at every turn. Unlike Montaigne, Machiavelli thought that with boldness and guile a virtuoso prince might outwit her for a while, if not for ever. This hope, of course, emboldens the prince to assert himself with all necessary means. In this script fortune explains away failure, and necessity excuses cruelty.

Not everyone chooses to believe this nonsense. If fortune is omnipotent, then there is no point in losing one's honor, or anything else of value, to pure chance. "We may commonly observe, in the actions of this world," Montaigne wrote, "that Fortune, to apprise us of her power in all things, and because she takes pleasure in confounding our presumption, being unable to make a blockhead wise, makes him successful, to spite the virtuous." In short, Machiavelli and his heirs are puerile enthusiasts in their confidence in virtuoso princes. Montaigne's passivity was the counsel of caution and not a false imitation of the tragic spirit of Greek drama. It was a selective, personal, and skeptical policy of damage control in the middle of a civil war.

Skepticism is an eminently reasonable reaction to the normally bellicose uses of the word *necessity*. For it is in war or prewar that necessity is generally called upon as a justification. It certainly is a hardy claim, one that has managed to outlast its mate, fortune, in political casuistry. Fortune turned out to be a poor cover for military incompetence. The trouble was that there were always people who were not taken in by the notion that our fate is in our stars. Richard II complains incessantly about what fortune has done to him, but Bolingbroke, Shakespeare, and we know that he has only himself to blame.[31]

Since the eighteenth century neither fortune nor necessity has gone unchallenged. Technology has greatly decreased the empire of fatality, while the shadow of Kant hovers over necessity. For what can be called necessary in political affairs? The instinct for personal and collective self-preservation may be taken as a force of nature and as such necessary. When people defend themselves against aggressors bent upon pure extermination, they have been forced to return to the state of nature where there is no justice, only a struggle for bare survival. How many wars are really like that in the first place? And how many such wars could be avoided? If we answer those questions honestly, it is clear that the necessity of self-preservation is rare and that a return to a state of peace is generally possible. This is scarcely a novel observation. It returns us to Kant and the elements of democracy.

For Kant the contrast was not between honor and necessity as it had been for aristocratic Montaigne. His was the democratic alternative between law and war, republican government and monarchical anarchy.[32] Both understood war well enough to recognize that the language of justice was wholly irrelevant to it. What can be just about an enterprise in which the innocent perish more frequently than the guilty and that is nothing but a test of strength and endurance, even if these contests are occasionally rule-governed? To be drawn into a war for sheer survival may be a misfortune that the victims cannot avert but it cannot be just.

The future of fate and necessity was in more elaborate doctrines than the bald reason of state that Montaigne and Kant confronted. For all its realism, necessity was able to reemerge only in the wake of far more fatalistic ideologies. Until recently, Marx-

ist and Darwinian philosophies of history reintroduced iron necessities into politics, which justified measureless slaughter. In America, even before Darwin's work was raped for racist purposes,
geographical and biological necessity doomed the native American population to "removal."

"In the present state of our country," the House Committee on
Indian Affairs forecast in 1818, "one of two things seem[s] to be
necessary. Either that those sons of the forest be civilized or exter-
minated." Nothing can be more revealing than Senator Thomas
Hart Benton's celebrated words on the same subject. "Civilization or extinction has been the fate of all people who have found
themselves in the track of advancing whites."[33] It was a necessity
he did not regret. These well-known samples of political necessity
should remind us that nothing less will bring us to total inhuman-
ity or a loss of traditional restraints. Can anyone forget the con-
straining forces of manifest destiny that led us into Mexico, Cuba,
and the Philippines? This speech by Rep. Samuel S. Cox of Ohio
in 1859 was typical: "There is a law from which no one can escape,
that the weaker and disorganized nations must be absorbed by
the strong and organized nations. Nationalities of inferior grade
must surrender to those of superior civilization and polity! The
Mexican races must obey the law of nature!" Even John Quincy
Adams thought that there were "laws of political gravitation."
"Cuba can gravitate only toward the North American Union,
which by the same law cannot cast her off from its bosom."[34]

Given the dates of these commonplace sentiments, there is no
point in pinning the blame on Darwin. The phrase *the survival of
the fittest* was simply added as an ornament to long-standing dispositions. Physical necessity was already in place to overcome
conflicting political urges and the by-no-means silent opposition
to these policies. Indeed, one may well suspect that it is in free
societies where there is vigorous opposition to warlike policies
that the argument of necessity is loudest, but that is not the case.
It is the staple item of ideological discourse everywhere.

Although necessity has always been the favorite word of foreign
policy specialists, they have certainly not monopolized its use.

Advocates of the free market have also found a place for it in their arguments. I am in no way judging the economic validity of these or any other economic doctrines, and I shall limit myself to considering only their political implications, specifically their notions of social necessity and injustice. The free market may, indeed, be as efficient as is claimed, but that does not mean all of its ill effects are above political judgment. They may be either unjust or unalterable misfortunes. Some may be a result of passive injustice or at least are not beyond human control; some may be too difficult or too costly to change, but expense does not constitute impossibility.

The greatest single limitation on our political options, according to the libertarian creed, is the inevitability of tyranny if we do not have a perfectly free market. Capitalism, Milton Friedman admits, is not itself sufficient to ensure freedom, as prewar Japan and czarist Russia show, but it is an absolutely necessary condition. American First Amendment rights are dependent upon the possibility of finding alternative employment when political fanatics fire us, which would be impossible if the government were the only employer. For the government is an agency of pure coercion, while the market is a system of "bilaterally voluntary and informed" transactions. If the government interferes with the latter, disaster must follow; there is bound to be a complete loss of prosperity and freedom. This conclusion depends more on the way the economy and the government—*any* government—are defined than on historical analysis. That is why it seems so necessary.

Society is held together by a delicate thread and any government that does more than secure property and set the rules of the game of the market is sure to invite a collapse of the balance of agreement. Such a disruption of tenuous social bonds will lead to a mad scramble of interests and end in chaos. Yet diversity is to be encouraged, which is far from dangerous as long as it expresses itself without resort to governmental activity. Certainly, if the social world is composed of two systems—one free, impersonal, and cooperative, the other oppressive, personal, and coercive—then it is necessary and inevitable that only the predominance of the former can prevent the triumph of tyranny.[35]

While there is an occasional reference to misfortune in Fried-man's books, his is not really a fatalistic vision, apart from the inexorable requirements of liberty that leave us with no political choices. To understand both the necessity of the free market and of the misfortunes it entails, one must turn to a remarkable book by Friedrich Hayek. In *The Mirage of Social Justice*, he heroically and clearly asks whether the misfortunes that the perfect econ-omy must cause can be regarded as unjust. While he is sure that this is not the case, he has certainly not evaded any of the difficulties of his position. In this he is, I think, unique.[36]

We need the free market or the "spontaneous order," as Hayek calls it, because of our irremediable ignorance. This is not the general ignorance that skepticism accepts. It is limited to our knowledge of market transactions. Individuals make their eco-nomic decisions in total ignorance of their outcome, for the latter depends on the behavior of countless other persons. We are ruled not merely by an invisible but by an unknowable hand. Neither statistics nor calculations of probability appear to be of any use in predicting the workings of the hand as it may affect us directly, not because we fail to think scientifically but because it is useless. We are left in the dark as we make our choices.

In spite of Hayek, social ignorance does not yield any specific inferences. There is no way of knowing what we would do in a state of perfect uncertainty, but the result is not likely to be a spontaneous, or any other, order. The most probable outcome would be paralysis, since the ignorant in their helplessness would engage in no projects, take few risks, and form no life plans. They would know the criminal law and what counted as prop-erty, but that would not be enough to give them a clue about their future. Having imperfect information, which is our real condi-tion, is very far from total ignorance, but neither great, little, or no predictability can itself bring about spontaneous and ungov-erned social cooperation. Ignorance imposes no necessity; it leads us in no particular direction, though immobility seems the most plausible.

Hayek's vision of ignorance, it must be repeated, is not a philosophical skepticism, such as Plato's or Montaigne's. It is highly selective. He believes that we do, in fact, know a great deal, especially about the course of our history. It is an evolutionary, cultural process in which individuals spontaneously and functionally adapt to changes in order to maintain the order of the whole. We know what is and is not functional, in short. The invisible hand is thus not just an explanation of complex social patterns that are the outcome of human decisions but not of explicit individual designs.[37] It can also be used to predict the future of the whole order. And it sternly points to the stiff limits of what is and what is not possible. In specific detail the operations of the hand are inexplicable, given our ignorance, but we can recognize the whole and predict accurately how it will behave in the future, especially if we do not obey its demands. The certain punishment for disobedience is tyranny.

The spontaneous order is a game of pure chance, and we cannot personally guess what to expect. All we need and ought to have are clear, general rules of personal conduct and ownership that make life tolerably predictable and maintain the game itself. This is the "rule of law" and it consists of general directives, like the rules of the road, but nothing specific. It is not, or at least should not, be deliberately made by human legislators. It has been the positivist's, especially Hans Kelsen's, unfortunately self-fulfilling prophecy that makes us actually legislate, rather than merely record, the rules that emerge in the integrative evolutionary process. The task of general rules is to help people to adapt to evolutionary changes that are not planned but are wholly spontaneous emanations of a multitude of individually blind actions.

Although Hayek has many harsh things to say about people who cannot shake off their inherited animistic superstitions, his view of law as a self-woven net is, as he recognizes, deeply traditional. In this he is not unlike Michael Oakeshott, who thinks that we can have a good society, but only if we leave government to people who have had a least three generations to acquire the habits of conduct required for the task.[38] For it does not call for skills or general ideas, just for an inherited capacity to recognize the intimations of one's society and to act upon those shared understandings. Such a government would know that it has nothing to distribute and therefore cannot be responsible for primary justice. Honors, offices, and wealth are not at its disposal. It merely reacts intuitively to the traditions of a people, not to fulfill any plan or achieve any specific results, but merely to allow everyone to pursue their chosen parts in a play that has no author and that appears simply to be *there*. If we do not accept the script as it has developed over time, we will face disasters, of which war and tyranny are the most obvious. That these were not absent in ancient Greece and Rome, nor in medieval England, is not mentioned.

This joining of traditionalist politics to free market economics is far from new. William Graham Sumner's *Folkways* was a highly moral account of the impossibility of altering social customs, and it was eventually written into our constitutional law in the Supreme Court's decision in *Plessy v. Ferguson* of unlamented memory. Not that Sumner lacked moral fervor. He thought that the market selected the virtuous for wealth and threw down the inefficient as they deserved. Millionaires were chosen for their work, and we all benefit from it. As has often been noted, his version of the invisible hand bore a close resemblance to the Providence of his Calvinist forebears.[39]

In his way, Milton Friedman echoes him when he warns us that although racism is "bad taste," it can be reduced only by social pressures, not by law, in a free society. Moreover, "we should not be so naïve as to suppose that deep-seated values and beliefs can be uprooted . . . by law."[40] The critics of the free market who object to its "atomizatation" of society within the spontaneous order, should find this traditionalism reassuring. The cumulative effect, given how rigid the rules of the game itself must be, is virtually to eliminate social choice. And in the realm of necessity it is absurd to complain of injustice.

It is not only that distributive justice is a "mirage," to use Hayek's term, injustice is a necessary and inherent part of the spontaneous society. When the established expectations of indi-

viduals are disappointed, they may well feel that they are suffering an injustice, but they are wrong. It is merely a misfortune.
Hayek specifically takes William Graham Sumner to task for
defending free enterprise on the ground that it rewards the deserving. According to Hayek, the market does nothing of the sort. Its
outcomes are morally entirely random. This is a fairly courageous
admission because there is ample evidence that the American
public supports the free market precisely because it shares Sumner's moralistic beliefs in the justice of its distributions, as Robert
Lane has shown convincingly.[41] The market is regarded as a natural order, and firms must, therefore, respond to competitive pressures. But as far as individuals are concerned, merit and hard
work are rewarded, and sloth and lack of education are punished.

The government, in contrast, is looked upon with profound
suspicion. There are many reasons for this, among which unfair
taxation is not unimportant. But common goods are not usually
counted, although private purchases are. No one buys the high-
way, just the car. Moreover, the government is always second when
it comes to dividing up the cake. It redistributes and disturbs a
state of equilibrium, so its actions are visible and subject to ethical scrutiny. No one knows how the original distribution occurred.
This point is stressed by Hayek. One can call a public agent unjust
because he or she is visibly responsible for his or her conduct,
but the market can never be just or unjust since it has no will and
no designs. To think of it otherwise is to give way to the most
primitive animism and to see a deity behind every natural disaster. Clearly, the American public is retrograde. For while it may
not share John Rawls's notion of justice, neither does it accept
Hayek's program. There seems to be no great preference for life
in an unjust and random society, even if it be free and productive.

It would, however, be entirely wrong to think of Hayek as
a latter-day Trevelyan. He is not interested in the moral self-
protection of the Victorian civil service. He does not blame the
poor for their poverty, pretend that they are better off than they
think, and that, in any case, everything that can be done for them
has been done. Nor does he claim that their situation is not only

necessary but also just. It is much to his credit that he does not yield to the urge to blame the victim. He even suggests that some victims ought to be helped. The truly helpless should be taken out of the market and cared for—but not by the government and least of all by a democratic regime. For public agents cannot be relied upon to limit their charitable efforts and to keep their hands off the market.

It is Hayek's emphasis on the misfortunes inflicted upon us by the market that distinguishes his book from others that share his views in general. He does nothing to sugar the pill. His market is neither fair nor unfair; it knows only winners and losers. It has no will, no purposes, no personality. We cannot hold it responsible for anything at all. Because the market is an impersonal force of nature, those who are injured by it cannot claim that they have suffered an injustice, although many of their normal expectations may have been shattered.

The sense of injustice has no place here, no more so than in cases of earthquakes or volcanic eruptions. The sense of injustice here has been wholly divorced from injustice itself and is treated as of no account in its own right. This is a necessary conclusion if we are truly doomed to ignorance about market operations that does not afflict us in other matters. Nor does the force of necessity weigh upon us as heavily in other realms. We have all kinds of technology and public programs to alleviate natural disasters and would consider it unjust if they were not used. But it is true that we no longer blame God for storms and, according to Hayek, should not blame the invisible hand for personal misfortunes either. He might have recalled that it is precisely because we do not look to God that we now expect and get public agencies to help and protect us from such disasters.

Perhaps theorists of economic necessity, like many technological determinists, especially Marxist, find the hand of fate as hard to bear consistently as most other people.[42] That would certainly account for the strain of conspiracy thinking that marks them. Conspiracy, like fortune, of course, accounts for failure, but it also puts someone in charge of an unyielding world. For Oakeshott it is the rationalists, the technicians, the self-made people who since Descartes have conspired to ruin traditional habits. Sometimes, however, he sees a more fatal flaw stemming from Stoicism and Christianity, which rejected the cultivation of suitable practices in favor of moral idealism. But if we are the victims of this moral misfortune, it is still the social engineers among us who are out to undermine tradition and good order and the habits that sustain them.

The government and occasionally the monopolists, especially the unions, are the true constant enemies; they do conspire to destroy our freedom, and much else. It is in fact a Manichaean world, which is ironic because the invisible hand as an explanation was originally meant to free us from irrational fears of conspiracy. But then it is a common observation of psychologists that most people prefer to see conspiracies rather than to recognize that no one is in charge at all.[43] It is proof of our need to blame and accuse, and Hayek is no exception.

The real message of the invisible hand is simple. Although it may yield many personal misfortunes, it yields no injustices. Our sense of injustice is irrelevant and the line between misfortune and injustice is clear and harsh. Nevertheless, this is supposed to be a rational world, one that moves to ever higher levels of civilization, of its own accord, and requires that we adjust to its historical requirements.

It seems to me that this is a poor argument because it is evident that when we can alleviate suffering, whatever its cause, it is passively unjust to stand by and do nothing. It is not the origin of injury, but the possibility of preventing and reducing its costs, that allows us to judge whether there was or was not unjustifiable passivity in the face of disaster. Nor is the sense of injustice irrelevant. The voices of the victims must always be heard first, not only to find out whether officially recognized social expectations have been denied, but also to attend to their interpretations of the situation. Are changes in the order of publicly accepted claims called for? Are the rules such that the victim could have consented to them had she been asked? If the victim's suffering is due to accident or misfortune but could be remedied by public agents, then it is unjust if nothing is done to help. A valid expectation has been ignored and her sense of injustice should assert itself and we should all protest. It is at the very least what one should expect of the citizens of a democracy.

If we look more carefully at injustice, we will not find it any easier to answer the question: Is this a misfortune or an injustice? on any given occasion, but we may be less passively unjust than if we simply match complaints against the rules and come to a quick conclusion. To investigate the victim's claims in the ways that I have suggested is only a tentative test to guide us, but it is both in keeping with the best impulses of democracy and our only alternative to a complacency that is bound to favor the unjust.

We might of course become so rational some day that we will cease to ask these questions, forget about responsibility, require no government, and just spread the costs of disasters, accidents and injustices indifferently. We would first have to learn to live in a random world, and we would also have to be without a sense of injustice. It is not an appealing prospect, nor a likely one. Until then, we can at least cry out with Voltaire, "Do not presume to soothe such misery / With the fixed laws of calm necessity."

3 THE SENSE OF INJUSTICE

When the victims of disasters refuse to resign themselves to their misfortunes and cry out in anger, we
hear the voice of the sense of injustice. Voltaire is
their poet. What, however, is the sense of injustice? First and foremost it is the special kind of anger
we feel when we are denied promised benefits and
when we do not get what we believe to be our due.
It is the betrayal that we experience when others
disappoint expectations that they have created in
us. And it has always been with us. We hear the
sense of injustice in the voices of Job and Jonah
and Hesiod at the dawn of our literary history, and
it still rings loud and true. Where indeed would
our literature be without it? What on earth would
Dickens have had to write about without the sense
of injustice? He, no less than Voltaire, reminds us
that we are not only aroused on our behalf but emphatically also when the indignities of injustice are
experienced by other people. The sense of injustice
is eminently political. In spite of all the difficulties
of knowing how to tell an injustice from a misfortune and who the real victims are, we know perfectly well what we feel, once we do recognize them.
When it asserts itself, the sense of injustice is un-
mistakable even when we refuse to acknowledge it.

THE DEMOCRATIC SENSE OF INJUSTICE

Although the sense of injustice has not gone unnoticed, it has not always played an important part in political thought and action. It is, after all, the specialty of the losers. Its political dangers were always known, to be sure, since yesterday's outcast may well be tomorrow's revolutionary avenger. And so, Aristotle noted that perceived injustice stimulates revolutions, but his interest in the subject was limited to its ideological expression. His successors were also ready enough to notice the unjust conduct of tyrants who violated the rules of primary and secondary justice only too frequently. They were the princes on whose behalf devils were depicted as beating up justice. In many cases, subjects were advised that they were not obliged to obey such a ruler. Their personal sense of injustice, however, played no part in theories that contemplated only monarchical and aristocratic governments. In modern democratic theory, however, the individual citizen's sense of grievance occupies the center of the stage, both as a psychological and a political concern.

In democratic thinking, the sense of injustice is taken to be an intrinsic part of our moral structure and an appropriate reaction to unwarranted social deprivation. The perplexities of inherently subjective and personal reactions to injustice also stand out more starkly in democratic thinking. When are they politically justified? How is one to respond to their promptings? Probably nothing can assuage the sense of injustice as well as revenge, which is incompatible with justice as it is normally understood. Moreover, though we tend to experience injustice in particular and individual instances, justice must of necessity be general and social in its aims. It does not simply negate and dissipate the sense of injustice to which democrats must respond positively.

If we recognize that ours is a world of irremediable inequalities, then we know that the sense of injustice and its sources can never be obliterated. Even in societies where equality is generally valued, there are bound to be advantaged and disadvantaged people, the strong and the weak, and these inequalities create the field in which the betrayal of hope and the sense of injustice flourish. However, even though inequality seems unavoidable, I shall argue that constitutional democracy does provide the best available political response to the sense of injustice. It does not, of course, put an end to injustice. Indeed, even the best political systems inevitably generate sources of resentment. At least democracy does not silence the voice of the aggrieved and accepts expressions of felt injustice as a mandate for change, while most other regimes resort to repression.

To begin again with some intellectual history. The sense of injustice as a fundamental experience plays a relatively small part in classical ethics. Apart from its place in political conflict, Aristotle did not dwell on it. It has only a minimal significance in his account of personal ethics, especially in comparison to modern democratic thought. There is nothing remotely comparable to the democratic notion of a universal sense of injustice to be found in Rousseau's or Tom Paine's political psychology. Perceived injustice fuels the struggle between rich and poor, according to Aristotle, but that is because they are locked into an ideological conflict about primary justice. He also mentions the righteous indignation that we feel at the sight of undeserved good fortune or unmerited misfortune, but that is only the mark of an ethical character and falls between envy and spite, which are excesses. The first is evoked by the well-being of others, whether it is deserved or not, while the latter rejoices at the suffering of others. Neither is an attractive trait, unlike sober and respectable indignation.[1] The latter is not a sense of injustice, however. It is too cognitive and unfelt, unlike the anger that anticipates the pleasure of revenge. Revenge, however, is not open to all but only to the free and noble.

In Aristotle's *Politics* only wounded honor comes close to a sense of injustice. Noble youths who have suffered some sexual indignity kill the tyrant who has offended their own and their family's honor. Wounded honor is, however, an entirely aristocratic disposition, and Aristotle presents it as such.[2] There is nothing universal about it. Noblemen are dishonored as members of a caste, but a democratic sense of injustice asserts itself when one has been denied one's dignity as a human being.[3] There is a vast difference between an aristocratic and a democratic ethos. One could argue that no aristocrat could possibly acknowledge a sense of injustice in all its fullness. If wounded honor calls for satisfaction, the democratic sense of injustice cries out for more, for a public recognition that it is wrong and unfair to deny to anyone a minimum of human dignity. In principle, therefore, democracy should respect the sense of injustice and grant it considerable scope. Ever since we became "created equal," all our claims are supposed to matter, and when they are disdained we are expected to protest in public.

To appreciate the full moral and political meaning of the sense of injustice, one had best turn to democratic political theory and its greatest representative, Rousseau. He was an injustice collector of genius, as well as the most profound of egalitarian thinkers. His works are a veritable museum of every form and variety of human injustice. Indeed, *The Confessions* proves that even bile can give rise to a remarkable work of art. As he saw it, the sense of injustice was a universal human disposition, an ineradicable social emotion and a politically significant phenomenon. And it is with us all the time thanks to what we do to each other. Perhaps one must assume with Rousseau that we can feel compassion for at least the physical suffering of all sentient creatures, if one is to give the sense of injustice a salient and not wholly self-regarding place in our psychic economy. In any case, without this ability to feel the pain of unjust slights, both one's own and other people's, the sense of injustice would not be, as it is, the core of the modern democratic political sensibility.

Rousseau's works do not slight the normal model of justice. Any society is by definition a system of rules that distinguish right from wrong and better from worse. Some people must be praised and others condemned.[4] However, any social inequality, even if grounded in moral judgment, creates emotional changes in us that will eventually make us both the perpetrators and the victims of injustice. It is thus in justice itself that the sense of injustice begins. For when we judge each other we immediately establish an inequality of esteem between us, and this distinction opens the door to others that entail dependence and oppression. Ultimately we sink or rise in our self-created hierarchy of values. Comparisons and any standard of measurement mean inequality and with it self-division for the individual and injustice between people. So vast and intense is the impact of the latter that one may hope for a palliative but not an eradication of the basic harm.

In every historically known society, the rich dominate the poor with the latter's hapless consent, since they accept their fate for the sake of peace. That is the real meaning of recognizing thine and mine and of the normal model of justice. Its roots are, moreover, within each of us. If people are given a rule to follow, they will at once learn to cheat and lie, to be consciously unjust. "With conventions and duties are born deceit and lying."[5] In a radically unequal society the rules cannot but encourage unlawful conduct among the deprived and their exploiters. The former are desperate, the latter can get away with it. Law naturally falls very differently upon them.

The normal model of justice is thus revealed as the expression of the inequality that is the real fountain and origin of injustice, which has an exuberant life of its own and which no system of justice, however fair, can ever expect to eliminate. The conventional view, moreover, does not even understand itself. For while we internalize the ethos of inequality and accept it as right and just, we do not lose our natural ability to feel deprived, humiliated, and offended when our expectations as human beings are not met, when our claims are ignored, when our sense of our dignity and all our sensibilities are affronted, and when we are despised and rejected. And many of our expectations are rooted in nature, not in culture. So deep is our sense of injustice that it embitters our lives day in day out. Most of us do not do anything about it and follow rules meekly, but that hardly improves us or our situation. Our sense of injustice may be dormant, but it cannot go away entirely. To have no idea of what it means to be treated unjustly is to have no moral knowledge, no moral life\

Rousseau was persuaded that the sense of injustice was natural when he observed an enraged baby screaming his heart out when his nurse hit him to stop crying. If an infant could be reduced to despair by an intentional offence, then surely the sentiments of justice and injustice were innate in the human heart.[6] His theory of education was to be built on that assumption. Emile, his imaginary pupil, is encouraged to plant some beans on a plot on which the gardener had already planted some fruit. When the gardener simply uproots the boy's beans, the child is enraged. "The sweet fruit of his care" has been wantonly destroyed and the sense of injustice is fully ignited in his little breast. He has also learned that his claim to his beans as his property was justified by the labor he put into growing them, and that injustice consists in depriving people of property so acquired. Unhappily, the gardener's claim is even better than Emile's, since he was there first. Eventually the two get together and agree to divide the plot between them and to respect each other's work.[7] Nevertheless, with the first experience of injustice, Emile has entered society and its rules, and he is no longer an innocent young animal but an intelligent and moral being. The world of vice is open to him as well now. The primacy and universality of the sense of injustice could scarcely be represented more effectively. Eventually Emile's education will take him beyond personal injustice to an understanding of politics, upon which everything ultimately depends.

Rousseau thought that the sense of injustice could endure not only as a reaction to personal injury but could, through social education, become an empathetic response to the injuries of other people as well. There is nothing natural about Emile's acceptance of the gardener's claim. He had to learn to do so, but had he not had the primary experience of injustice in the first place, he would not have come to terms with the rights of others. Rousseau thought that it was important to teach children their rights first, so that they might eventually grasp their duties when they are ready to understand that other people also feel the stings of the sense of injustice, which is the natural ground of our rights. He certainly was able to convince his many readers that a sense of injustice was the one universal mark of our humanity and the one natural core of our morality. It is our most basic claim to dignity.

It is thus not surprising, given Rousseau's enormous impact, that since the eighteenth century the sense of injustice and its associated emotions, frustration, anger, and fear, have been of enormous concern to psychologists of all kinds. Thanks to their findings, it appears that although retaliation in response to an injury, immediately after the act, is known among many animals, planned revenge is not. Fear and rage, moreover, involve known physiological reactions, which animals can feel no less intensely than we do.[8] What is it that sets the sense of injustice apart from the pure frustration that animals also feel when they are denied something they usually get? The best suggestion is that from an early age we learn from the experiences of others by making comparisons and forming an idea of what we ought to expect under prevailing standards, however vague these may be.[9] Above all, we recognize the difference between socially validated expectations, mere fantasies, and unwarranted hopes.

The English language is of some help, moreover, in showing us the difference between ourselves and our animal friends. The latter, no less than we, expect *that* something will be done because it always has been done, as effect follows cause, and if it is something we enjoy, they and we are sorely disappointed and frustrated if it fails to happen. People, however, also have expectations from or of each other, and these depend upon our roles and the social character of our mutual relations. We expect fairness *from* public officials, fidelity *from* our friends and the delivery of goods and services *from* those we have paid for them. We feel betrayed, not just upset, when these expectations are not met. Statistics may tell us that this is probably going to happen, but that hardly makes us feel better. A black American may well expect *that* she will not get a fair hearing from certain public agencies, but as a citizen she knows that this is not what is expected *of* our public servants, and she can certainly feel and communicate her sense of injustice when her claims are ignored.[10] There is, however, a bond between these two kinds of expectation. Unpredicted, sudden injustices are resented far more intensely than those one has learned to endure as a member of a group. They tear away the emotional protection created by resignation and allow distress to burst from its confines.[11]

For the personal sense of injustice to come into play fully there must be some ground for feeling that a disappointment is not merely an unpleasant surprise but a deliberate or avoidable injury. One must at least suspect that one is not merely unfortunate. And this intuition deserves public respect. Since there is no clear answer to the question of who determines whether an expectation is authoritatively legitimate and politically recognized or just seems to be subjectively so to a mistaken or merely unconventional complainer, it is impossible to come to a plausible guess without hearing the claims of sensed injustice carefully. If one regards the sense of injustice as Rousseau did, as innate and naturally accurate, then one must, at least initially, credit the voice of the victim rather than that of society's official agents, of the accused injurer, or of the evasive citizens. Given the inevitability of the inequality of all kinds of power among us, it is the necessary democratic response. The claim may be unfounded on the available evidence and might be rejected, but the putative victim must be heard. Hers is the privileged voice because hers is the one voice without which it is impossible to decide whether she suffered an injustice or a misfortune.

Democratic theory does not have to attribute an identical sense of injustice to all people. All that has to be asserted is that normal human beings can tell when they have been affronted. Under reasonably favorable, democratic political conditions, their sense of personal dignity will flourish and be encouraged to assert itself, especially against the chronic arrogance of governmental agents. Ideally, citizens should be protected not only against injuries but also against being pushed around for "their own good." Moreover, without their overt consent and understanding, we have no reason to suppose that their legitimate expectations are being met and that their silence implies anything but resigned acceptance.

THE VOICE OF THE VICTIMS: "REVENGE!"

It would be childish, however, to imagine that democratic attitudes and institutions constitute an adequate response to the sense of injustice. It is not even plausible. The procedures of consent may be the best we can do, but they do not conquer the dominion of injustice. No political system can satisfy the discontents and differences that the social condition creates within and between us. No one can eliminate conflict and dishonesty, and the restraints of the criminal law have psychological limitations, in addition to their obvious practical inefficacy. Most important, the spontaneous reaction to injustice is not a call for legal procedures, but for revenge. A sense of injustice not only makes us boil quietly, it also moves us to get even, for it does nothing to make us more rational. This realization emerged when the sense of injustice became universally interesting in the eighteenth century.

To illustrate the point, one might consider the work of one of Rousseau's eighteenth-century disciples, Dr. Itard. As he reported to the appropriate governmental agency, he had tried to teach a wild child, found in the woods, not only to speak but also to behave morally. He was, however, not sure whether he had merely modified Victor's behavior or awakened his moral sense. To test him, he locked Victor in a closet, which was his usual punishment, but this time the boy had in fact behaved well. When the enraged child was released, he bit Itard's hand. The doctor was completely delighted because this act of revenge proved to him that Victor did indeed have "both a sense of injustice and a sense of justice" and was thus a full human being.[12] It was, he noted, an entirely legitimate act of revenge. In provoking it, Itard felt he had raised the savage to the full height of a moral being. Victor now possessed the most decisive characteristic and the most noble attribute of social man, for these two sentiments were the eternal basis of the social order. For Itard, as an ardent environmentalist (more so than Rousseau), the important point was that justice, like everything else, was learned. Both, however, believed that we know our rights even as children or idiots and that we manifest a sense of injustice when we resort to primitive acts of revenge, as did the wild boy.

Not everyone would recognize Victor's conduct as sufficient evidence of a sense of injustice. John Stuart Mill could accept revenge as only part of a full social consciousness that recognized the supreme utility of justice and was aroused impartially as much by injustice to others as to oneself. The sense of injustice could count only as part of a fully worked out intellectual and morally mature understanding of justice as a social necessity. The mere feeling did not signify. But then Mill was not a particularly democratic thinker, as his contempt for the less than fully educated majority shows clearly enough. In his view, most people could not be trusted to report more than their animal reflexes, and these were of no great account until they had been evaluated by the more competent few.[13] For Rousseau and Itard, however, anyone who could feel that he or she had suffered an unmerited injury and could respond to it intelligibly had demonstrated a capacity to understand injustice. Nothing more was required for moral maturity.

Indeed, Rousseau believed that simply to be conscious of injustice proved that one was a moral being. More radical than Itard, he did not regard the urge to take revenge as a necessary moral trait. The pure feeling of injustice, which, he was sure, we had from the moment of our birth, was enough. Personal experience had taught Rousseau that the unjustly punished child might never say or do anything at all in response. He may even develop, as he himself had, a taste for being subjugated. Such a child does not lose his moral consciousness, nor does a burning sensation of defeat and anger go away.[14] Everything we have learned lately about the victims of domestic abuse and violence confirms Rousseau's observations. We also know now, as he did, that this too is ultimately a political issue. He was therefore far less interested in personal revenge than in education and in democratic reform. Emile is not allowed to do what Victor does, to take the law into his own teeth. He is taught to be totally independent of other people and thus outside the reign of inequality and of potential and actual injustice. If he were ever to become a citizen, he would not be passively unjust but would do his best to prevent the abuse of private and public power.

Victor's story is, however, more plausible than Emile's. Revenge is an insatiable urge of the human heart. Victor's bite was a natural response to an implied promise or at least to an expectation that Itard had fostered. Like most acts of revenge, it was a personal reaction to an intentional offense that violated shared and acknowledged norms, in a moment when no appeals to an umpire were possible. *Free revenge* may occur either because there are no public agencies available or because no illegality is involved, as in the breaking of a personal promise. Sometimes there may be no appropriate institutions in place, at least temporarily, as in the Wild West. Not everyone resorts to self-help in these circumstances; those who do find that it gives them satisfaction as nothing else can. Bacon called revenge "wild justice" precisely because it is a real passion.[15] It is not eradicated in any political system, which is why democratic theory cannot afford to ignore it.

Individual, hands-on, direct revenge is not the only way to avenge injustice. There is vengeance, which is a social or religious obligation. Then there is social retaliation, which has the more general aim of attacking public wrongs. Unlike these, revenge is uniquely subjective, not measurable, and probably an unquenchable urge of the provoked human heart. It is the very opposite of justice, in every respect, and inherently incompatible with it. Even if legal justice must, to some degree at least, satisfy the vengeful urges of the injured and their friends, it cannot succeed consistently. Revenge is not detached, impersonal, proportionate, or rule-bound. And it is because of its disorderly nature that, as Bacon thought, the law must weed it out. The past, he went on to reason, cannot be undone by another injury, after all.[16] But then neither does justice wipe the slate clean. Revenge at least equalizes the wrongs and repays the wronged person with the pleasure of making those who have treated him unjustly suffer for it.

If effective justice preempts, neutralizes, dilutes, and all but replaces revenge, it cannot abolish it, either as an emotion or as an active response available to us, especially in personal relations. For most people retributive justice *is* justice, but it remains a frustrating substitute for revenge, neither eliminating nor satisfying its urging.[17] Moreover, the sense of injustice is as often ignited by injuries that the official agencies of justice cannot touch. A broken private promise or a personal betrayal may fall entirely outside the law, but some people will do something about it. There is the famous Balzac story, for instance, about the husband who bricked up the door of the cupboard in which his wife's lover was hiding, while she watched. Not everyone has such opportunities. What can a child do about a gratuitous promise that has been broken? Nothing much, except nurse a sense of injustice. Among equals the hurt may be lighter. People in business write off broken informal promises as a normal cost of doing business because it is neither a personal slight nor an issue of power. Revenge may occur here, but it does not seem to be common.[18] Personal betrayal, however, smarts, and if there is an opportunity to get back at the offender, the temptation for the sense of injustice to express itself in revenge is powerful. Unlike justice, revenge meets the specific case directly, indifferent to every other concern except the need to react to an insult or a perceived wrong.

Obligatory vengeance is not like revenge. It is a social duty to avenge one's kin, as a rule, and it may have nothing to do with the wishes of the individual who is obliged to do it. Orestes did not want to kill his mother, but he had to avenge his father and, in any case, was acting out an inherited curse. Having done the deed, he is in turn pursued by the Furies who must now avenge the murder of his mother. Only when Athena intervenes and transforms them into happy spirits who administer civic justice is the endless cycle of vengeance put to an end. It is thus that in

Aeschylus's *The Eumenides* civic harmony is achieved only when the goddess breaks the fatalism of inherited curses and regulates the duty to avenge one's kin.[19] Hamlet also laments that he is being forced to put things right by avenging his father. He does not really want to kill his uncle, and when eventually he does so, he is sacrificed in the act. It is young Fortenbras, again an outside force, who puts things in order in Denmark. It is this sort of self-help by kinsmen that the institutions of justice are meant to replace, control, and destroy. To the extent that vengeance is a caste code, it is not easy to break down. Dueling in defense of one's honor was difficult to abolish, as is the vendetta.

The vendetta is a more egalitarian form of vengeance. It is also a culturally imposed duty. It still rages in Corsica because the state is not strong enough to stamp it out. Here the sense of injustice is not aristocratic but irremediably anarchic. The cost of the distrust and fear that haunt these familial societies is enormous. Here personally delivered justice as a private enterprise creates so pervasive a sense of distrust and suspicion that economic and social development are impossible in this morally paralyzed society.[20] While revenge and its pleasures appear to play a part in the vendetta, vengeance is not a matter of individual choice here either. Like the slaughters of avenging kinsmen, vendettas are apt to be interminable.

Finally there is political retaliation, which occurs when a personal sense of injustice resorts to public action in response to political injuries. It is an exceptionally complicated notion because each instance is unique, depending on the historical situation of which it is a part. Historians tend to ignore the part that personal experiences of injustice and resentment play in rebellions and revolutions, but novelists have been more perceptive. We need go no further than *A Tale of Two Cities* to see these passions at work.

Dickens is not alone. There are two tellings of the same fable that brilliantly illuminate the translation of intensely felt personal injustice into political violence. The hero of Heinrich von Kleist's *Michael Kohlhaas* and Coalhouse Walker, who is at the center of E. L. Doctorow's *Ragtime*, live in remote ages and circumstances, which make all the difference in the meaning of their otherwise identical experiences of political injustice. The first lives in a society that is said to be generally just, and Kohlhaas is subjected to an exceptional outrage. Coalhouse lives in unjust, racist America at the turn of the century. Except for their time, place, and color, they are meant to be the same man.

In the age of Luther, a Junker unjustly confiscates and abuses Kohlhaas's two horses. Kohlhaas expects to get speedy justice but finds out that no one will listen to his suit because the young nobleman has important connections at court. As he pursues his case, he is subjected to endless insults and injuries until he finally raises a peasant band that terrorizes the whole neighborhood. In the end, however, justice does prevail. The good Elector of Brandenburg goes over the whole record, puts the Junker in jail, restores the horses to their owner, and sends Kohlhaas's sons to the school for noble pages. The Imperial authorities, of course, demand that Kohlhaas be executed as an outlaw, a judgment he readily accepts as his due. After all, he did get the justice he demanded in the end. He also gets revenge because the man who had betrayed him all along, the Elector of Saxony, desperately wants a piece of paper that foretells his fate, which Kohlhaas manages to obtain and swallow in front of his distraught enemy's eyes. Assuming no irony on Kleist's part, this is a story of justice vindicated because a just political world of law-enforcing princes is taken for granted, even by Kohlhaas in his fanatical quest for personal vindication. Here social retaliation, even though violent and anarchic, is a form of public protest that ceases as soon as one man's sense of injustice has been satisfied.

That is not at all the world of Coalhouse Walker, the black jazz pianist. When his Model T Ford is vandalized by a racist fire chief and his men, no lawyer will take up his case. He too gathers a band of youths that burns stations and shoots a few people. When the youths occupy the Morgan mansion in New York, the authorities finally intervene and make the fire chief repair the car and apologize to Coalhouse. Coalhouse gives himself up, as agreed, and is shot by the police as he walks out the door. This is where the similarities between the two stories end. Neither Coalhouse nor his followers think that they live in a just society or that any-one in officially racist America would ever treat them fairly. Coal-house's young followers want him to organize a social rebellion, rather than seek a merely personal vindication. They did not fight to get him his car back and an apology; they want their rights as citizens to be recognized. Coalhouse, perhaps because he is an artist, is too aloof and solitary for social rebellion. He may also realize that it would fail and bring untold suffering to black peo-ple. In any case, like Kohlhaas, he simply pursues his own griev-ances, but there is no good prince to set things right for him. In his world there can be no just ending, because his real enemy is an entire society.[21]

What of Coalhouse's followers, one white, the rest black, who want to move on to revolutionary violence? They have no hope of justice or fair treatment in an unjust and violent society. They might well choose the satisfactions of politically futile but manly retaliation, whatever the cost to other black people. In any case things cannot get worse, they might claim. There is not much one could have said to them then, except that things can *always* get worse.

What if these young men had taken to ideology? What might they offer as an ideological justification for continuing their ram-page? First, they could claim that no killing of whites is indis-criminate in America, since all are implicated in the practices and benefits of racism. In addition they could say, having now read Jean-Paul Sartre, that violence is cleansing and liberating, and that it alone can transform them from victims into free men.[22] Killing the oppressive "other" is in and of itself wholesome and restorative. As there is no psychological evidence for this propo-sition, it might well be put aside, but that would be a mistake because what it does describe is the emotional gratifications of immediate physical retaliation. It makes no political sense, but it certainly does remind us of the exhilaration of revenge. We should also remember that this romance of violence cannot alter the fact that the habits of retaliation acquired in war and revolution are not conducive to eventually decent government.

The argument that no one is politically innocent is, however, more interesting. For it is framed in the language of justice and appeals to its principles. It is by these that it must therefore be judged. Retaliation, it is claimed, is a just punishment of those who deserve it, and everyone without exception in an oppressive society does deserve it. In this verdict there is no measure of relative guilt and no proportionality in punishment, such as even the rougher forms of criminal justice demand. The appeal to justice therefore fails because this is, like every other form of revenge, "wild." What the accusation of universal guilt does invoke successfully is the ideology that governs all modern wars and revolutions, "Those who are not for us are against us."

If the charge of universal guilt could mean anything at all, it would have to refer to passive, not active, injustice. However, the crime that every inhabitant of an oppressive society is being charged with is not Ciceronian passive injustice, but simply being part of a social whole. Good citizens should, indeed, have paid more attention to the political issues presented by racism, taken active sides, and in general should have been better informed and more vocal. But a just citizen might have come to the conclusion, on the balance of the evidence, that Jim Crow was best because that is what most of the certified geneticists and his political leaders told him. It was also what he wanted to believe. He would have decided that being black was a real misfortune, and most of his fellow citizens would have agreed with him. Being a good citizen is not the same thing as being wise, unbiased, humane, or unusually independent. No such claims can or should be made for citizenship. Rousseau was on solid ground when he noted that the best citizens were xenophobic and bellicose. Passive injustice is a civic failing, not a sin or a crime. It refers to the demands of our political role in a constitutional democracy, not to our duties as men and women in general. Common sense and history tell us, moreover, that reigns of terror do not teach civic virtue, but its opposite.

Nevertheless, the fact remains that Coalhouse and his followers were not the victims of misfortune but of many injustices, which they could do very little to end. Coalhouse grasped that fact tragically. If his young band chose to continue shooting, it was revenge and not justice, the logic of war, not of right, because there is no just way to overcome many of the realms of injustice. Retaliation certainly has its appeal, but it is not punishment or reeducation. The choice of whether to resign oneself to iniquity or to fight it by any available means is not, therefore, one that can be defended in terms of the normal model of justice. Certainly, the charge of undifferentiated, universal guilt is even politically irrelevant, since after all we are all guilty of something. Men oppress women, adults oppress children, and so on. We are both victims and victimizers, and so we may, presumably, all kill each other. This ghoulish version of original sin is not a political idea.

Even though the terrorists' vindication of retaliation is untenable, it is not aberrant in the extreme. Indeed, it is most conventional. Most just-war theorists in our age of nation states also argue that the citizens of an aggressor state are to some extent implicated in the criminal guilt of their government, and that while there are limits to what one may inflict on civilians, they cannot be protected against most of the military consequences of belonging to such states.[23] It does not excuse terrorist acts to note that terrorism does not differ from the collectivist ideology of nation-statehood. By incorporating all citizens into the state, this nationalism also holds each one indiscriminately liable for the acts of those who happen to govern them. The wages of modern warfare are their just deserts, it is said. Since this is what church and state preach, the idea of collective guilt is the common understanding of our age, not just the rage of a few crazies. One might, of course, argue that it is an ideological curse that we have inflicted upon ourselves.

Coalhouse's putative terrorists would, certainly, have as plausible a defense as any for turning political retaliation into a war of liberation, a "just war." And we should not depoliticize their conduct by labeling it "narcissistic rage."[24] If we reject that excuse, then their violence would have all of Bacon's wildness. Like most acts of retaliation, it would not cancel the original offense, would not appease their anger but would only turn it into repetitive, new channels. However, although retaliation may be uncertain and random, it is obviously a most rewarding way to express the sense of injustice, directly and personally, even if it is self-defeating in the long run. Terror, like personal revenge, may on occasion give satisfaction but like any war, it is hardly a sure thing.

There are obvious democratic objections to retaliation as well. Overwhelmingly, war works in favor of the strong and against the interests of the weak. That, as it turns out, is also one of its greatest philosophical attractions. For the shadow of Nietzsche hangs heavily over all the dreams about noble avengers. The superman would rise above it, but the Greek nobility did not, and they at least were healthy. The move from heroic to civic justice took away the nobility of it, according to Nietzsche, and democracy is just the last step in an unabated decline. Originally justice was a matter of paying one's debts to one's equals. If a debtor broke faith, the creditor might avenge himself or make a public spectacle, a festival of cruelty, out of the debtor who had exposed himself to such a fate when he failed to keep his word. Such justice can exist only between equals, and for Nietzsche that meant the real equality of noble caste members, not the fictitious equality of legal persons.

What we normally call injustice cannot be ascribed to Nietzsche's defaulting noble debtors. Only those who fear and resent them call them unjust and, with the aid of priestcraft, they have been able to make the charge stick. The ordinary sense of injustice is merely the lingering resentment of the victorious herd. The ability of the strong to enforce mutual promises has been curbed, and they are constrained lest they threaten the sleep of the weak. The vengeful and the civic senses of injustice thus have two entirely different genealogies. The first arises out of private agreements between powerful and potentially vengeful equals; the latter out of the fears of the feeble and their priests.[25] In the Nietzschean view, public justice represents the victory of the weak and their sense of injustice. It is merely a mixture of envy and fear or, to use his word, resentment.

This vulgar historical myth amounts to a simple assertion that the agencies of public justice are inevitably the forces of a leveling ethos that caters to the herd's sense of injustice. Its heroic pathos is essentially a nostalgia for Orestes' fate-haunted Greece. One might well ignore it if it did not enjoy so great an appeal in spite of its complete irrelevance to any organized political society. Its psychological force among the literate who are drawn to it must lie in its chief claim—that nothing can replace direct revenge for those who are strong enough to enjoy its risks, and many of Nietzsche's readers obviously do imagine that they might rise to that noble challenge.

In spite of all that can and has been said on behalf of revenge, Athena was surely right when she replaced it with civil justice. Established institutions of justice allow us to say that justice was done far more often than revenge allows us its satisfactions. They are infinitely more reliable in every way in settling disputes and punishing criminals than are the various forms of revenge. Yet they seem to give us far less pleasure. Given the intensity with which we experience the sense of injustice, why do we not appreciate legal justice wholeheartedly, nor rejoice in its efforts? After all, it is our most sensible resort. Why does justice as continuous lawful conduct seem to cause us so little gratification? Perhaps there is no physiological response to the calm enforcement of the rules, whereas the frustration of denied expectations, rage, and fear involve physical reactions as well as moral ones. The absence of injustice causes mild contentment when we think of it at all, but when we fail to get what we know to be our due, we react strongly. We know that justice as a policy cannot achieve all we would want it to, but surely—considering how rare and precious active public justice is—it should do better than it does in our political affections. In fact, it cannot compete with tradition, nationalism, and xenophobia in stimulating our political loyalties. Like revenge, but unlike public justice, these also give immediate pleasure. Somehow injustice and justice are not psychologically complimentary or symmetrical, nor are they exact opposites.

Giotto, *La Giustizia*, Cappella degli Scrovegni, Padua. Courtesy of Alinari/Art Resource, New York.

PUBLIC JUSTICE AND ITS DISCONTENTS

Another look at Giotto's pictures in the Arena Chapel can tell us much about the disparity in the intensity of our responses to injustice and justice. As we turn from the image of Injustice to that of Justice, which faces it on the opposite wall, we cannot but become aware of the emotional difference in their effect upon us. The two pictures are dissimilar, but not really direct opposites of one another. Justice is a calm and majestic woman who looks right at us, not at either the heaven or hell of the Last Judgment. She may not be a real person at all, as Injustice certainly is with his lupine face. Her face is benign. But apart from that it is expressionless, as one might expect of the impartiality appropriate to a personification of justice. We can certainly feel afraid of Injustice, but Justice radiates no emotional appeal.

Perhaps Justice is a benevolent ruler or simply the queen of all virtues. Behind her is a lovely arch in perfect condition. In her right hand is the minute figure of a winged victory that is being sent to a man at a bench who is either reading or working. In her left hand is a tiny Jove with a thunderbolt going to a beheading, to a person about to be executed. Giotto's Justice does not use a scale; she weighs directly with her own hands, implying that she is indeed justice entire, in no need of instruments to help her. She also does not seem to require the aid of Christian faith, since her messengers, Nike and Jove, are obviously classical and pagan. Her activities are clear: virtue is rewarded and crime is punished. Presumably there is no occasion for revenge here.

As with Injustice, the consequences of Justice are to be seen at her feet. There are two hunters, two men dancing, one with a tambourine near a small hut, and two others standing at their ease. What it says is that Justice lets people enjoy themselves, but she does not direct them to any public ends. People can relax even in the woods. Nothing is to be seen that implies private or public wealth, nor earnest citizens engaged in political deliberation, nor cooperative endeavors. Without that scene of good times the picture of Justice would not give rise to any feeling, except the knowledge that crime does not pay here and that work is rewarded. Hardly stirring emotions!

Giotto's Justice is at least not blindfolded, since this peculiar way of ensuring fairness had not yet been invented.[26] She does not, however, look at the objects of her reward and punishment, and they do not arouse her or our feelings in any way. Unlike Injustice, she is not passive; she is clearly doing something as she gives each his or her due, but if not cold, she does come across as tepid. And although Injustice arouses fear and revulsion, Justice suggests repose and security. But the match of positive and negative attributes is no longer clear at this point. Are dancing and hunting really the obverse of murder, rape, and theft? Security from attack may allow us to do these things, and just government does make us feel less threatened, even if not perfectly safe, as the fact that a criminal is being executed suggests. Should there be more?

The normal response to justice may be a feeling of enhanced security because those who govern are meeting ethical standards and performing their official responsibilities. It is a means, not an end in itself. The desire for safety is not foolish, and a law-bound government is the least threatening form of social control. If citizens hope for an end to crime, governmental agencies at least do not add to their fears but reduce them by demonstrating their support for justice, even if crime is not eradicated.

The positive activity of Justice as she punishes and rewards, no less than her appearance, puts her outside the world of her dancing and frolicking beneficiaries. It is not she directly, but the ease she ensures that creates pleasure in the picture. That points to another disparity between Giotto's two figures. Injustice is not only odious in and of himself but also prunes the trees that grow in the soil of iniquity. He and the criminals at his feet share a world. Justice, in both her appearance and actions, is wholly apart from her leisurely subjects as she distributes secondary justice in order to secure entitlements and punish the disorderly. She will certainly put some of our sense of injustice to rest, but we should expect more: an active political life.

The reason we may feel no joy in contemplating Giotto's Justice is that she calms our fears but thwarts our highest aspirations, whether they be heroic or civic. To a noble anarchist, Giotto's Justice may appear insipid because she is not dealing out heroic vengeance. Her calm face is remote from anything so disruptive and personal. She countenances measured retribution, not revenge. It does not add to her attractions in the eyes of the avenger within each of us. If she cures the sense of injustice, it is to avert self-help, which is incidental to her main task. She lacks the emotional punch that Injustice delivers and that revenge would also offer us. Giotto's Justice is also not a perfect response to the nightmare of his Injustice in the eyes of a democratic admirer of his art. For any politically organized society, the quality of justice depends crucially on the character of government, both in its structure and its actions. Giotto's Justice, unlike his Injustice, leaves the character of government in doubt. We know all about the public and private life of those Injustice encourages and rules, but what of the public experiences of these frolickers? Crime will be punished and work rewarded. Certainly Justice cannot be tyrannical, but there is no sign of Ciceronian republican or modern democratic values here. The citizens only play. They do not deliberate, vote, or administer. The queen does it all, handing out whatever is to be distributed, while the citizens are politically completely passive. In contrast, the subjects of Injustice are active partners in the moral or, to be exact, immoral life of their dreadful polity. They and their ruler are all of a piece. Justice is different. She hovers above her carefree beneficiaries.

In the Ciceronian view, on the contrary, justice is primarily a citizen's virtue. That is why he argued that wisdom without justice can do nothing, whereas justice without wisdom can achieve much. Most of us are not wise, but we can be just, and because real justice depends on decisions made by all citizens, it alone binds communities together, while injustice tears them apart.[27] This is scarcely a Platonic view, except in one respect. Government is meant to be active, not passive. Only the just conduct of individuals can create the trust that is indispensable among republican citizens who must decide such basic political issues as what counts as private property and what counts as public property. It is the necessary condition for republican government. Giotto's Justice does not seem to be doing enough for Cicero's citizens or, for that matter for Augustine's fallen humanity, not to mention Plato's new men.

Both a Ciceronian republican and a modern democrat would want more positive signs of civic activity. They do not mean to underrate security and leisure, which only a few of us have ever been able to enjoy, but they are not the same as political partici-pation. Nor is a carefree life a complete answer to the atrocities of Injustice, for though the citizens are clearly happy, they remain the dependent subjects of a queen. In any historical world it is doubtful that any regime can remain just if its citizens cannot take an active part in its public life. The sheer inequality between rulers and ruled is too great. There are many bureaucratic regimes that certainly follow the rules and are utterly predictable, and some are undeniably just. A Hegelian state, run by an impeccable universal class, would be just by any standards in administering existing rules fairly. The rule of law would be secure thanks to its upright public servants. Nevertheless, the many citizens relegated entirely to civil society would burn with a sense of injustice because they were not recognized as citizens with a right to gov-ern themselves. However, the absolute validity of political change in response to a public sense of injustice is not built into their orderly system of justice. In contrast, democracy must, as a mat-ter of principle, listen to the voice of protest, hear it out, weigh its message, and move, though it often acts with maddening torpor.

In the end, the entire effort of even benevolent rulers, and they are rare, is directed at keeping themselves in power and their subjects obedient. The latter are secure in their expectations, which have, however, been reduced to a miserable minimum. What they get and fatalistically expect is that punishment and reward will be administered punctiliously. The limits of the per-missible are rigid but well known. This is not arbitrariness, and it does constitute a very high degree of security. Even islands of personal pleasure can be created in such societies, such as we see in Giotto's Justice. But once the possibilities and ideologies of liberal democracy have spread, these regimes are perceived as restrictive and are resented. For they allow no genuine possibilities for creating, expressing, or asserting expectations other than those allowed by the regime. That is what political inequality means, and it is unjust.

The most drastic democratic way of dampening the sense of injustice is to allow the citizens to make the rules, but also to socialize the citizens so completely that their private aspirations will never diverge from public goals. That means a transformative education, which we can safely assume would not be acceptable to most U.S. citizens. Instead, they expect public justice to maintain the stability of a political order that cannot and will not validate aspirations that seem too radical. Some may be officially recognized at some point in the unpredictable future; many others will come to nothing. In actual political life there is no way to avoid a huge gap between the personal sense of injustice and established norms. Some claims will never seem to be anything but absurd demands, while others will appear obviously just in retrospect. In reality, the valid sense of injustice belongs to those who can prevail.

Consider again the sense of injustice felt by women. It has been around for centuries and centuries. "Women are not by any means to blame when they reject the rules of life which have been introduced into the world, seeing that it is the men who made them without their consent," wrote Montaigne, many years ago.[28] Not that he proposed to budge. Clearly, this man knew that the rules imposed on women were not made or enforced to suit them, nor were they in the interest of women or subject to their critical review. Yet women's sense of injustice did not count. It was at most a nuisance, not socially significant. Some women simply did not know how to accept misfortune gracefully. When rather recently the entrenched public definitions of what women have a social right to expect changed, it was because the feminist movement had become a major force in U.S. politics. That made the old rules officially unjust, thanks to female persistence, ideology, and the changing distributions of social power and inner dynamics of a democracy. This is a case of a validated sense of injustice. What of all the women whose sense of outrage went unheard and unnoticed for so many years? They were treated as eccentrics who did not understand scientific reality or the accepted rules. Being isolated and without political influence or standing, their voices were not counted.

The political point of this bit of history is not that democratic governments work slowly, but that democratic principles oblige us to treat each expression of a sense of injustice not just fairly according to the actual rules but also with a view to better and potentially more equal ones. To be sure, democracy does not fulfill its immanent promises quickly, but at least it does not silence the voice of protest, which it knows to be the herald of change.

It is, of course, impossible to list all possible forms of inequality and the feelings of injustice to which they may or may not give rise, but some do stand out, especially the failure to keep promises. Broken promises are interesting because they are as common in private as in public life. In both cases they are often acts of the strong against the weak, insults by the person who can either fulfill an expectation or deny it. The best way to think about promises is to place them in a continuum, depending on the relation between the people involved. At one end of the spectrum we would have the casual business promise that is routinely ignored by both parties, and at the other end we have promises made to someone who is emotionally and materially entirely dependent upon the promisor. The degree of inequality between the parties, in this view, largely determines the intensity of the sense of injustice that broken promises would inspire. It also reveals that the meaning of a promise cannot be grasped without listening to the disappointed person. In democratic politics his or her voice is especially significant because the broken promises of officials may well be acts of public wrongdoing, denials of legally recognized rights, or general failures to perform civil duties. In these cases the sense of injustice has serious political implications. For individual anger may become public distrust if its rightful claims are ignored, and its eventual consequences are not insignificant. The failure to live up to political promises enfeebles representative government and encourages political cynicism and passivity, as a failure to vote and refusal to report crimes show most notoriously.

Yet in spite of politicians who habitually break their promises, it is not to be feared that American citizens will lose their faith in the authority of the laws quickly. Their trust survives even though their suspicion of the government in general is enduring. In fact they may be too slow to react. There is substantial evidence that most people's cognitive bias toward preserving confidence in established institutions is considerable. But when people are made to see a specific instance of injustice, they will alter their long-held convictions. General statements do not have a great effect on people's cognitive responses, but one sensational example will move them.[29] We get angry at and on behalf of individuals but are indifferent to wrongs that seem to affect too many people at large. Adam Smith was on sound psychological ground when, to illustrate this very point, he cited the fact that people are ready to hang a murderer, but pity the sentinel who is shot for falling asleep at his post, even though the crime was a serious social offence.[30] That is why unjust court decisions rankle more than unfair laws. They generally afflict an individual litigant, not a faceless group.

Undeserved or excessive punishment, arbitrary or incompetent judges, delays, prejudiced juries, overly zealous public prosecutors, bribed lawyers, irresponsible witnesses, the litany of things that can and do go wrong is endless. When a court falls into disrepute because of corruption or incompetence, the sense of injustice is doubly ignited, which is why nothing causes greater outrage and indignation than justice sold and bought. Procedural unfairness, especially in court or in courtlike institutions, is excoriated as the very essence of injustice by Americans. And the failures of retributive justice in individual criminal cases are particularly resented.[31] When tribunals lapse from their legal duties, they fail totally. Not surprisingly, our literature is full of court dramas. They focus entirely on individual lives.

Miscarriages of procedural fairness are not, however, built into the principles of the legal process, except in one respect, the inability to deal with individuals as they really are rather than as legal persons. The injuries we experience are specific and concrete, whereas courts as agents of the law must remain general and abstract in their decisions, enhancing our sense of injustice occurring in the very act of being just. That is why our sense of injustice is not always appeased by fair decisions.

As Hume shrewdly noted long ago, we are exasperated when a bigot or a miser inherits a fortune while a prudent and generous person may be impoverished by prodigal parents or a foolish and spiteful will. This Hume thought was unreasonable on our part.[32] Enforcing valid wills is what a court is supposed to do, and it is the scheme as a whole, not the particular outcome, that is both just and benefits all. But although the purpose of justice in general is abstract, every unjust act is particular, as is the sense of injustice. Giotto's Justice and Injustice are not perfectly matching opposites or negations of each other because they are true to life. Perhaps the sense of injustice in the United States is atypical in its intense individualism, and one ought not to generalize, but those two pictures speak to us across centuries and political cultures. They seem to have been painted for the instruction of all citizens.

It is, nevertheless, wise in speaking about injustice to stay close to home, and I shall limit myself to the United States and its citizens. We are not, obviously, all of a piece, but social scientists in many surveys have come up with remarkably similar accounts of the beliefs of Americans and their sense of injustice. What stands out most is their absolute concentration on individuals in making judgements. Philosophers, the law, and the social sciences generalize, but citizens cling to the concrete. It is widely agreed that it is unjust to pay disproportionately much or little for work, but this is seen as an individual, not a social fault. So also is failure to do well. The existing evaluation of economic standing and the inequality to which it gives rise are not seen as unjust. Inequality is accepted and therefore only those cures for poverty that aim at helping specific individuals are acceptable. Training for greater opportunities is approved since it opens doors to individuals, but across the board redistributive welfare is unpopular.[33] On the other hand, in politics egalitarian standards prevail. Everyone is to have equal access to political agencies, and the use of money and influence to achieve political ends is regarded as unjust. Rights to legal services and office must be as equal as voting, the primary political act.

Not only merit, but need also constitutes a claim on us as persons and as citizens, but people disagree about how great the need must be; the more physical it seems, the more compelling it appears. It would be unjust to let someone die because she could not pay before being admitted to a hospital. That may, however, be more a matter of compassion than justice.[34] There is certainly a lot of disagreement about where the line is to be drawn in any specific case of need, and people differ in their sense of its injustice. Racism and arbitrarily blocked opportunities are the two general injustices that are widely recognized as such. That is what the word discrimination means, that someone has been deprived of a right on fraudulent and untrue grounds. The two most common principles of justice, need and merit, are not so much at war here as deployed as the occasion seems to demand. Sometimes need determines who is to get what; at other times it is merit. It depends on which is more obvious to the naked moral eye, which as a rule sees policy in a personal way.

Relative deprivation in America tends to be a personal reaction, aroused when someone pretty much like oneself gets something one also wants and feels equally entitled to. In more deeply class-divided societies, feelings of group and collective relative deprivation may be more common but excepting racial discrimination, it is a personal phenomenon in America.[35] That does not imply indifference but an intense individualism that recognizes that our many different roles entail their own obligations and rewards. This is remote from the passive submission to tradition and convention that is urged upon us by a self-congratulatory pluralism. For the multiplicity of roles, as perceived by Americans, never eliminates the primacy of the suffering individual or of the citizen as a discrete person.

What is dreadful is that even when people feel that they have suffered an injustice, they are apt to say and do nothing because they cannot hope for support from their peers or expect any success. That is the obvious reason why we may never really know the extent of both the injustices and the sense of injustice that prevail among us. Much is silent, forgotten, or locked away, which allows us to resign ourselves to them. Philosophers recognize their inevitability and citizens are no less ready to endure and inflict more injustice than they know they should—because it is our fate. Americans do react quickly to individual cases of injustice but put up with social unfairness. How could it be otherwise? Social information just dribbles in, bit by bit, and we simply get used to it. A single story about a person really hits home at once, but the grinding injustices of daily life are endured. It is easy to ignore them and we do.

Ideally, as democratic citizens, we should not wait until there are grounds for complaint, but Americans do not seem to have high political expectations. They look askance at all of government. Their pervasive distrust and cynicism have their public costs. To be sure, no one ought to trust any government implicitly, but the conviction that the government is at worst hostile or at best indifferent to the interests of ordinary citizens is not a cheering one. It is an unwholesome state of mind for the citizens of a constitutional democracy. For even if most of the sources of our sense of injustice are unquenchable, it should be the mark of a constitutional democracy to aspire to reduce them. We need a certain balance between trust and suspicion.[36] The difficulty is that even when justice and fairness do prevail, they are undramatic and forgettable, while injustice is always felt keenly and memorably. There does not seem to be any obvious way to maintain a realistic level of both distrust and confidence.

Given the normally personalizing thrust of the sense of injustice and our native individualism, it is not surprising that most citizens point to specific acts by public officials, judges, and civil servants when they think of typical injustices. Felt injustice is a personal experience, and it is evoked by particular incidents, which does not mean that it has no public implications, as citizen distrust of government amply shows. But it adds up to only a collection of attitudes, not to a public philosophy. We are not natural philosophers, and there is an enormous difference between the ways in which most American citizens and philosophers think about justice and injustice.[37] Contemporary American philosophers, like their predecessors since classical antiquity, mostly discuss *distributive*, or to be more exact, *primary* justice and injustice and the general political principles that would constitute a just society. They dwell on *macrojustice*, assuming the role of legislators as their own. When they consider injustice, it is only as a general political problem.

PRIMARY INJUSTICE?

What place does the sense of injustice have in the philosophical schemes of primary justice? The most convincing reasons for supposing that primary or political justice serves to eliminate felt injustice are to be found in Aristotle's *Politics*. Given that any city is composed of rich and poor citizens, there is bound to be an ideological conflict about what is due to whom. As a political emotion and a revolutionary ideology, the sense of injustice comes into its own here. For Aristotle it is significant as class resentment, pure and simple. The rich will say that honors and offices should be distributed in proportion to the wealth of each citizen. Since wealth constitutes merit, the rich should get more political power than the poor. Most citizens are, however, poor, and they think that freedom, not being a slave, is all that counts, and that all citizens should receive equal shares of honor and offices since all are equally free members of the city. Decisions should be made by a majority of voters, and equality is to prevail.

Utopia excepted, the most stable regime, according to Aristotle, is one in which each side compromises and checks the ideological ambitions of the other. A large class of middling fortunes is helpful, especially as the rich are individually so ambitious and their values inherently so competitive that they are unreliable as a governing elite. The object of mixing ideologies and classes is not, however, merely to avert coups and civil wars. For the mixed regime contrives institutionally to inhibit the greed of contending parties, and since Aristotle thought that greed was the sole source of unjust conduct, it is a regime that is genuinely and solidly based on relatively just, ungreedy conduct.

In this picture of primary justice, injustice is indeed curbed because the disposition that gives rise to it is checked by institutional pressures. The political sense of injustice and its disruptive ideologies also remain dormant. There is no free riding in what is a body of fair-minded, self-controlled citizens. It is not perfect government, which would improve the citizens far more, but it is not unjust in the way that rulers who care only for their own self-interest are.[38] Ambition checks ambition, in the Madisonian version of this thought. It is neither a noble nor an extensive notion of justice, and it makes sense only if one assumes that greed is the sole motive of injustice. If fear and aggression are taken as equally serious dispositions toward unjust conduct, then one can easily imagine rich and poor ganging up on groups or individuals in their midst with no regard for justice at all. Aristotle concedes as much in his account of ostracisms, few, if any, of which can have been deserved. Then there is aggression, perfectly acceptable against noncitizens, that is foreigners, metics, women, and slaves. But then they and their sense of injustice do not count for Aristotle.

Nevertheless, rich and poor are expansive notions, and we can easily see them dividing the entire population of a society, not only its free males. While greed is not the only cause of injustice, it is certainly not insignificant. With that in mind, it is fair to say that a relatively egalitarian version of Aristotelian political justice should succeed in reducing the sense of injustice. It need be neither restrictive nor oppressive. It becomes so only when justice as a ruling ideology is not defined clearly as an accepted mix of the openly and freely expressed aspirations of rich and poor citizens but merely as the prevailing set of "shared social meanings" that are read and interpreted but that are not tested by asking the least advantaged members what they actually want. These inti-mations of shared meaning, as divined by prophetic or tradition-alist avatars of the spirit of the people, are never checked against actual opinions, least of all those of the most disadvantaged and frightened people. To confuse a common culture with a harmony of political interests amounts to little but a sleight of hand. What cultures share as a rule is language, which makes it possible for us to express, among other things, our hatred and contempt for each other, as well as our sense of injustice, if we are not too cowed to do so. In the absence of a clear and free account of their feelings, we should assume that the least advantaged members of a society resent their situation, even though—like many a black slave—they smile and sing in a show of contentment.

For an inquiry into the preferences of the oppressed to mean anything at all, one would have to conduct it under conditions that make it possible for the most deprived members of society to speak without fear and with adequate information. How else can one know whether they really share the values of the masters? Historians indeed know that they have not, but that is retrospec-tion. Here and now there is no substitute for consent under con-ditions that make it genuine. Otherwise Sambo is the real self of the slave, and every domestic slave enjoyed washing the kitchen floor because that is what a woman was meant to do, and she thought that she could not do anything else. They all were per-fectly satisfied with the lines in the cultural "text" they were com-pelled to read, or to be exact, to endure.[39]

This is not to deny that ideologies and beliefs largely deter-mine what individuals regard as unjust. Thus most Orthodox Jewish women do not consider their position of inferiority to men at all unjust. We can be sure of that, however, only in America, because they have every opportunity to change their minds and leave their religious community if they wish to do so. As far as anyone can judge, they have consented to their roles and quite happily it would seem. If they had no choice, we would not be able to even guess their feelings.

There simply is absolutely no known alternative to consent

and especially to constant opportunities for dissent and exit under the most open and easy conditions. Nothing could be more deceptive than to impute contentment and assent to people who do not protest and to assume that, because the deprived and injured share the "meanings" of their society with their masters, they accept the conditions of their servitude. We know the history of slavery in America too well to need to be told that black people did not agree to it and that many knew perfectly well that it was unjust. Nor did they accept Jim Crow as anything but an unjust fate. There are many ways of accepting and rejecting the vast variety of social customs and usages in a pluralistic society, but they are open only to those who are audible in public. In the absence of realistic opportunities for choice, voice, protest, and denial, its rules are nothing but incentives to injustice. Especially as long as there are ascriptive groups that are not voluntary, the absence of consent is in itself an injustice. There is nothing just about a communal identification that one may not leave at will and that may doom one to social inferiority or to an unwanted social identity. Not to be asked at all whether one is really in favor of or against the arrangements that control one's life is to count for nothing, to be a zero.

If primary justice is wholly a matter of enduring local customs that are shared by all, especially in the absence of politically meaningful dissent and complaint, then the South's case for slavery was as just as any. In fact, the best case made before the Civil War was not that slaves had always been recognized as property and that the rights of property were sacred to all American citizens. It was that abstract justice was socially meaningless, that the entire culture and social fabric of the South entailed slavery, and that even the republican virtues of its citizens were dependent upon it.[40] Most communal politics throughout history have been so oppressive that under their determination primary justice distributed slavery and social disenfranchisement to most people by simply not counting their voices or allowing them an exit. Such justice also yields the compliance of the downtrodden, for it is fear and deprivation and the lessons they teach, not false consciousness, that account for their share in those common social meanings. Why should they pretend that they also count for anything in a caste society? And why should self-satisfied observers not believe that the prevailing ancestral relations are not those of trust created by bonds of mutuality? I do not choose to mention terrorist regimes with their concentration camps because they merely overdramatize the obvious. But does anyone still believe, as so many experts on China once claimed, that the Chinese enjoyed Mao's rule because that was what their culture had conditioned them to appreciate?

Clearly, no democrat can accept a system of primary justice that simply silences every expression of the sense of injustice. There are, however, other less drastic ways of constricting the legitimacy of the sense of injustice that seem less objectionable. One can limit the right to be heard to a small fortunate group. That is the pattern of Aristotelian thought, which makes all but a few master-class citizens inaudible. It is their misfortune to be unalterably inferior. The other way of reducing the legitimacy of grievances is to accept officially only a few complaints. That was Hume's solution. It depends on reducing the scope of primary justice radically. Dr. Johnson provided the rationale for that in his famous couplet, "How small of all that human hearts endure / That part which laws and kings can cause or cure." That sentiment would gain greater force if we admitted that it was only half true. Laws and governments can and do cause a great deal of human misery. And what they cause they can avoid and ameliorate. Dr. Johnson, however, had the immensity of suffering in mind.

The advocates of minimal government do not dwell on its impotence in the face of our suffering. They simply define justice narrowly, thus leaving little for government to do. Misfortune is correspondingly expansive. Justice demands only that we abstain from injuring our neighbor and their own. That is why justice is the least of the virtues, according to Adam Smith. Accordingly, resentment was for him a purely personal response to a direct assault on one's property or body.[41] Any other sense of injustice was idiosyncratic. Hume's "cautious and jealous" virtue also can have no other end in view than to secure ownership and avert violence. In effect, this notion of justice is simply peace, and it attends to only those perceived injustices that have been ungenerously defined as acts of overt violence in the first place. Though their reasoning was different, these ideas clearly are the precursors of Hayek's fatalism.

We often choose peace over justice, to be sure, but they are not the same. To confuse them is simply to invite passive injustice. Inactive government is not only abusive in individual cases when the weak and vulnerable are left to their fate. It also enhances such gross inequalities of social status and wealth as to make the denial of access to courts, legal services, and police protection the rule rather than the exception. Informal promise breaking in matters of wages and other basic expectations, and physical exploitation would be normal, and opportunities for education and health would be regarded as not a matter of justice but of fortune. It is only by relegating most of the objects of justice to fate that Hume's and Smith's stringently defined primary justice can be said to function at all. Most unjust acts are simply redefined as misfortunes, which is a notion many people are only too prepared to accept, as we have seen. Nevertheless, a passively unjust political system has not been tolerable to the long-suffering majority of European and American citizens, who resorted to democratic systems of government.

In reactions against these narrow and pinched views of primary justice, there are now many democratic alternatives that are as inclusive as possible. They look not only to greater equality but also to a legitimization of as many social claims as possible. In America, reforming theories of primary justice have certainly not ignored the importance and value of freedom and consent, though some involve troubling provisions for perpetual public moral education based on dubious psychological theories. There is no denying that greater equality of power would enhance the conditions for justice, but many of the plans offered for its achievement are flawed. The single most serious objection to them is not that they are radical but that they are often so paternalistic as to arouse a sense of injustice. Though they aim at a more perfect democracy, plans for the reform of existing institutions often require remaking the citizenry as well. And who exactly is competent to do so?

Even the modest reformers in contemporary America, where technology has created huge differences between the ignorant and the informed, are tempted to administer people as if they were things, without offering them an explanation. Paternalism at present begins with a view of the poor as so defective as to have no understanding of their own welfare. Only those who hover above them, and perhaps over society as a whole, can really define and impose justice. Justice is, like Giotto's queen, not one of us. In reality, however, unlike Platonic philosophers, one cannot begin with a clean historical slate to redistribute wealth here and now. And the citizenry are not psychologically made of clay. They not only deserve explanations for the rules that alter their lives but must be assumed to be able to understand them. Nor should one forget that if one really understands a subject, however complex, it is generally possible to explain it to almost anyone who wants to listen. Most social policies are not all that complicated in any case. To assume imbecility is as unjust as one can imagine.

Paternalism is usually faulted for limiting our freedom by forcing us to act for our own good. It is also, and possibly more significantly, unjust and bound to arouse a sense of injustice. Paternalistic laws may have as much consent as any other, but what makes their implementation objectionable is the refusal to explain to their purported beneficiaries why they must alter their conduct or comply with protective regulations. People are assumed to be incompetent without any proof. The result may be entirely just, but the treatment of the "clients" is not. Welfare recipients who receive benefits in kind rather than money are simply presumed to be incapable of understanding their own interests, "noncompetence is assumed until disproved."[42]

The cognitive inequality between the agents of the state and their clients is taken to be so great as to be unbridgeable as well as permanent. Whether they are to receive medical treatment, be relocated, or given benefits in kind and monitored for compliant behavior, they are never owed nor do they receive an explanation for what is being done *for* them.[43] That the agents of the state should get into the habit of playing God is in itself offensive, though the decision to redistribute wealth was in itself entirely just. Again, injustice lurks in the pursuit of justice for all.

It might be rightly argued that as a picture of redistributive justice this is a caricature. It is, however, by no means an inaccurate account of what is done in the name of welfare. Paternalism is not, however, the only occasion of the ambiguities of just reform. There is an inevitable dissonance between even the fairest of public reforms and established private expectations. Almost every new law, however benign, displaces someone's expectations and plans and arouses their sense of injustice, often violently. That is why in constitutional governments laws are passed slowly and in public, so that individuals can adjust their plans to new legal conditions. Every social change, every new law, every forced alteration of public rules is unjust to someone. The more drastic and sudden the change, the greater the grievances. That is not meant to be an argument against legislated change but a recognition that it is not simply a cure for the sense of injustice but, on the contrary, one of its many sources.

Henry Sidgwick already noted that common sense ethics has no answer to the tension between two types of justice, the conservative that meets entrenched social expectations and the reforming that wants laws to meet newly arisen ones demanding political change.[44] Sooner or later one side will feel and express a sense of injustice. At some point even relatively just social reallocations will seem massively unjust when they involve too many people in extensive upheavals and disruptions. Just as surely, postponing the changes demanded by socially conscious groups and interests will yield its harvest of indignation and protest. In politics, common sense is by far our best guide, but it does seem to lead us into a complete impasse.

Ideological and moral changes may demand altered primary allocations, but it is never a unanimous or painless process. To redress one injustice is to create another. Every new tax law seems and feels unjust to those who planned their lives on the basis of existing law. Every change in the admission rules to a university disappoints a group that had grown up expecting to be admitted. Planned inflation that redistributes income by melting away the savings of old ladies is not self-evidently just, neither are deflationary policies and lowered wage earnings. All these policies can, however, be defended as acts of primary justice if they are in keeping with new ideological commitments, additional material resources, or technological changes. Unavoidably, they also create a sense of injustice among those whose law-created expectations have been blown away. For years every official and unofficial authority had told them that their existing powers and possessions were theirs as a matter of right. Why should they not feel injured when they are suddenly told that this must now end? Even if it is reinforced by massive reeducation for similar future policies, just reform is often too equivocal to be regarded as merely an elimination of existing injustices. There are limits to what reform can do to lessen a sense of social injustice in society as a whole. To realize this is not to argue against political change but to grasp the inevitablity of incompatible political values and the necessity of procedures for trading them off as we go along.

If one looks at the conflicts between types of justice and injustice not as single instances but as a process of mutual accommodation, however, the picture improves politically. The best way to bridge the gap between settled expectations and demands for public change may be a system of effective and continuous citizen participation in which no one wins or loses all the time. That is the promise of democratic politics, and again one can recognize it in Rousseau's *Social Contract*. In his account, the individuals who are about to form a polity already have a sense of injustice because they are not alike in strength and possessions and because they are in grave danger of being fooled by the rich into selling political equality for peace. This is what has, in fact, happened at all times and in almost all places. Instead they stop short of that abyss and bind themselves mutually to create general and fair laws under which they will all be equally protected. The sense of injustice to which we must fall victim under every other system of law is thus discharged forever. Unhappily, the costs of this system are unacceptable to sane people. For the citizens must internalize these laws so deeply that they need feel no distance between their private and public lives. They must be transformed.[45]

Nevertheless, Rousseau's idea of continuous consent as a way of overcoming the discrepancies between personal and public justice remains an essential aspect of any democratic ideal. Participation may not cure us of neuroses, as many American participatory democrats claim. And the Spartan rigor of Rousseau's polity is certainly not what most urban Americans want. Nor can we afford to release all our aggressions upon foreigners, as Rousseau suggested. Modern representative democracy calls for far less intense or immediate acts of consent, but it does share his deepest hope: to be our own masters.

Stripped of its imaginative excesses and reduced to the possible, Rousseau's proposal for uninterrupted deliberation about the rules of primary justice is at least a plausible way of reducing the sense of injustice that must attend legal change. Consent as a continuous process under conditions of personal freedom may well be the only way we know to avoid laws that doom us to a recurrent sense of injustice. It does not abolish the latter or the occasions that give rise to it, but it does allow us to do something about them, and it creates the hope that they will be altered. Citizens can, moreover, expect that on some other issue and on some other day their preferences and beliefs will prevail. You win some and you lose some. Though not transforming, the politics of consent and dissent in constitutional democracies narrows the unbridgeable gulf between a personal sense of injustice and public laws that might change too slowly or too quickly.

What if inheritances will be outlawed or taxed far more heavily than they now are? While I had planned my life on the assumption that I would be rich when my parents died, and I borrowed some money, I now find myself unable to pay my debts. I am, however, an incurable reformer and regard inheritance as a violation of the American promise of equal opportunity. I therefore do not rejoice, perhaps, but I do not feel that I am the victim of injustice. My siblings, however, feel both ideologically and personally affronted. They have read Robert Nozick with enthusiasm and they are enraged. Their sense of injustice is not an irrational reaction to acute personal disappointment but like most public sentiments, it can and has been philosophically defended.

What can they do to alleviate their sense of injustice? If they protest it will do them little good, though it may relieve their feelings, and in a free society they will not be punished for expressing their grievances. They can do something to defeat the members of Congress who voted for the law that deprived them of their inheritance and possibly try to challenge the law in the courts. But it is clear that their consent to our condition is not like mine. They have agreed only to a process of government and while it makes their loss more bearable, it would simply be untrue to say that, especially given their ideology, they have not been treated unjustly.

Nor should we discount the private upheavals caused by a sense of injustice created by new laws. We have quarreled so much that we no longer talk to each other. Lately, however, things have improved. Predictably, I saw only disaster in referenda that mandated caps on property taxes, but my siblings supported these measures and won. We now get on well. Nevertheless, there is no way of imposing a judgment upon all of us. In determining the validity of one's sense of injustice, one is one's own judge. The best claim one can make for democracy is that it narrows the distance between self-evaluation and public judgment, but no regime can close it.

Who can tell us that we have no right to feel injured when we think that we have been treated unfairly? We live under rules and laws not of our making or in our interest. And if we belong to a condemned ascriptive group, we may have to put up with discrimination. That this may last for a long time hardly improves the situation. Tradition is often nothing but the evidence of silence. And the acceptance of defeat cannot be taken as consent, even when one is not threatened with jail for complaining. Is the consent of those who, like the libertarians in my story, have agreed only to a process any better? Have they really consented to anything at all? Surely the answer must be yes. Procedural justice is not merely a formal ritual, as is so often charged. It is a system that in principle gives everyone some access to the agencies of rectification and, more significantly, the possibility of expressing a sense of injustice to some effect, at least occasionally. To be included is to have social standing. The demands of procedural rectitude in voting, legislating, and judging, moreover, are not psychologically or ethically empty either. They create their own characteristics of forbearance and propriety as well as forcing the restraints of fairness upon public agents.[46] Unlike the excluded, those who can take part in these procedures can advertise their grievances and point a finger at the offending party or state of affairs. They can come back to recoup their losses because they are not politically voiceless.

There is, however, no reason to suppose that procedural fairness as a means of allowing citizens to consent and dissent is a cure for a sense of injustice. Even perfect procedures can be grossly inequitable in specific cases, especially when their aims are forgotten, ambiguous, or simply irrational. It is a point often illustrated by lotteries. They are usually established with the consent of all the participants, and they are utterly fair. Everyone has an equal chance. As a way of disposing of unclaimed property of no great value, it is surely the perfection of justice. What, however, if the object is less benign and an abandoned child is raffled off? After all, no one chooses one's parents, and natural birth is a pretty random process. Adoption, however, is neither physiologically nor socially like natural parenthood, and to pretend that it is as fortuitous is simply not true. We would still think that Solomon was wise, even if we were not sure that the better mother was necessarily the biological one. Solomon wanted all the relevant facts about those two women before making his decision. He was not gambling with the child's future.

The fact that the parties to the lottery consent to a completely irrational procedure does not make it acceptable. They do not, after all, believe as some Greeks did that the gods decide. They are simply leaving it to pure chance in order to avoid conflict and discussion. The avoidance of an unjust outcome is not one of their concerns. Clearly, the injustice to the child is manifest since its welfare is simply ignored and it is not given to the most suitable parents or chosen by them directly. The relation of injustice to indifference also stands out as a form of fraud, since from the first there is a refusal to consider all of the relevant facts about the available families. But then willed ignorance is at the heart of passive injustice. That is why irrationality is itself a source of injustice and one against which no system can always protect us, especially when, as in lotteries, it may have benefits such as peace and quiet.

Lotteries are, for all their apparent fairness, deeply fatalistic; they circumvent the uncertainties of deliberation and voting. It also appears that people dislike them when significant objects are to be distributed. Lotteries offer macrojustice, but pure chance is felt to be too irrational for the purpose. No procedure so indifferent to individuals is satisfying.[47] Lotteries are also typically one-shot affairs and in this respect entirely unlike the continuous procedures of democratic government. What they do illustrate is how, at its worst, an excessive and mindless submission to procedures can produce enormous iniquities. The procedures of representative democracy do not have to be like that. They can impose thoughtfulness and deliberation upon us, which allow us to prevent the arbitrariness that may find its way into pure procedural fairness and the injustice that lies within justice itself. Nevertheless, laws properly enacted and fairly administered are responsible for many of our feelings of injustice. They are not misfortunes but injustices we cannot or will not avoid.

How resigned should we be? Should we listen to those who tell us that we do not have all the facts, lack public experience, and are not as far-sighted as our elected and appointed officials? Should we accept the official story that we are the victims of misfortune when we think that we have been subjected to injustice? All public agents are alike in one respect: all have a wealth of excuses for the resentments they create. These are too familiar to be listed, but they are usually invocations of circumstances, unavoidable error, or just a shifting of blame. Necessity seems to fence them in on all sides when they are asked to face the injustices for which they are directly or passively responsible. What their litany of evasions does reveal is a dreary moral and linguistic uniformity. People who worry too much about moral relativism might well ponder that; for agreement has not made anyone less unjust. In any case, it is not in the choice of principles but in coming to political decisions about what to do in specific instances that American citizens disagree most frequently, as indeed they always have.

Do we give up too easily? Stalemates, cross-purposes, diversity of aims, and diversions are all the results of freedom, and all can and do induce indifference, fatalism, and passive injustice. "Life is unfair," we say, and think of something less painful. But should we? How much is inevitable, and how much injustice is due to human choices and agency? When should we give free expression to our sense of injustice, and when must we simply pack it up? What is bad luck, and what is unjust? It has not been my purpose to draw a line between them, since it is the argument of this book that no such line can be drawn in general or abstractly. Whatever decisions we do make will, however, be unjust unless we take the victim's view into full account and give her voice its full weight. Anything less is not only unfair, it is also politically dangerous. Democratic citizens have the best chance of making the most tolerable decisions but certainly not always, given the extent, variety, and durability of human injustice.

NOTES

INTRODUCTION

1. To social scientists it has long been clear, to quote Mary Douglas, that "the line between natural and man-made causes is always drawn in a social process of allocating responsibility." See M. Douglas, *Risk Acceptability according to the Social Sciences*, Russell Sage Foundation, New York, 1985, esp. p. 26. Not everyone thinks like that, however, and many friends have suggested that I ought to indicate that I am aware of the cultural partiality of my own views and do not merely take the fact of diversity for granted. Clearly, I discuss justice and injustice in the context of a society in which political and legal equality are widely accepted cultural values, which might not be the case in a hierarchical society. See, e.g., André Béteille, *The Idea of Natural Inequality*, Oxford University Press, Delhi, 1983.

2. See Lawrence M. Friedman, *Total Justice*, Russell Sage Foundation, New York, 1985, for an exaggerated but not unwarranted account of the legal aspirations of Americans to find a way to right every wrong.

3. See Dennis F. Thompson, *Political Ethics and Public Office*, Harvard University Press, Cambridge, 1988, pp. 40–65, for a severe stance on the dirt on "many hands," which I share, but perhaps for different reasons.

4. *DeShaney v. Winnebago County Department of Social Services et al.*, 57 *U.S.L.W.* 4218 (February 21, 1989). I would like to thank Martha Minow for allowing me to read her

very valuable unpublished essay, "Law and Violence," on this case.

5. I owe the phrase "parajudicial conception of morality" to Joel Feinberg, *Doing and Deserving*, Princeton University Press, Princeton, N.J., 1970, p. 85, and I would like to acknowledge a debt to his writings that is far greater than any number of footnotes could ever express.

6. This is true of even the best of the legal accounts of her and Pickwick's relations, and one for which I am in other respects much indebted to P. S. Atiyah, *Promises, Morals and Law*, Clarendon Press, Oxford, 1981, pp. 146–48.

7. As an example, see again Atiyah's certainly brilliant book *Promises, Morals and Law*, esp. pp. 212–15. The difference between his collectivist and Charles Fried's individualistic view of promises, which does concentrate on expectations, is no part of my subject, since Fried also considers only the "objective" claims of the parties created by promises. See his *Contract as Promise*, Harvard University Press, Cambridge, 1981, with which, however, I do agree.

8. See, e.g., Annette Baier, *Postures of the Mind*, University of Minnesota Press, Minneapolis, 1985, pp. 174–206, who alone takes the victim's point of view into account, though her main concern is a defense of Hume's theory of promises.

9. There is a wonderful account of Pickwick's education in W. H. Auden, *The Dyer's Hand*, Vintage Books, New York, 1968, pp. 407–32.

10. Jean-Jacques Rousseau, "Sur l'économie politique," *Oeuvres Complètes*, vol. 3, Pléiade, Paris, 1964, p. 246, my translation. Also, J. N. Shklar, *Men and Citizens*, Cambridge University Press, Cambridge, 1969, pp. 92–93.

CHAPTER 1

1. Dennis E. Curtis and Judith Resnik, "Images of Justice," *Yale Law Journal* 96 (1987): 1727–72, for an account of the many representations of justice as they appear to lawyers.

2. There is one brief but notable exception, from which I have learned much: A. D. Woozley, "Injustice," *American Philosophical Quarterly*, monograph 7, 1973, pp. 109–22. On the other hand, Barrington Moore's *Injustice: The Social Basis of Obedience and Revolt*, M. E. Sharp, New York, 1978, in spite of its title, has no bearing on my subject. Its concern is with the reasons for the failure of Marx's predictions about the social beliefs and conduct of the working classes. Whatever interest that topic may have in its own right, it is irrelevant to this book.

3. See Quentin Skinner, *Ambrogio Lorenzetti: The Artist as Political Philosopher*, The Raleigh Lecture, Proceedings of the British Academy, vol. 72, 1986, for a perfect account of one of these conventional representations.

4. To see how very much alive Aristotle's model remains, see, e.g., Charles Taylor, "The Nature and Scope of Distributive Justice," *Philosophy and the Human Sciences*, Philosophical Papers, vol. 2, Cambridge University Press, Cambridge, 1985, pp. 289–317.

5. John Stuart Mill, *Utilitarianism*, J. M. Dent, London, 1944, pp. 38–60.

6. See Friedrich A. Hayek, *Law, Legislation and Liberty*, vol. 2, *The Mirage of Social Justice*, University of Chicago Press, Chicago, 1978, pp. 162–64, for a full list of references to passages on injustice as the motive for thinking about justice.

7. The following discussion of Plato's devastating account of legal justice is based on *The Republic*, tr. and ed. Allan Bloom, Basic Books, New York, 1968, bk. 2, 369a–373e, bk. 3, 405a–405d, bk. 4, 421c–426e, 442d–445d.

8. David Sachs, "A Fallacy in Plato's Republic," in *Plato*, ed. Gregory Vlastos, Anchor Books, New York, 1971, pp. 35–51; and Mary Margaret Mackenzie, *Plato on Punishment*, University of California Press, Berkeley, 1981, pp. 153–55.

9. My account of Augustine's doctrines is based on *The City of God*, tr. M. Dods, Modern Library, New York, 1950, pp. 681–90, 692–93, 699–701.

10. Ibid., 681–83.

11. Michel de Montaigne, "Of Coaches," "Of the Art of Conversation," "Of Cripples," "Of Physiognomy," and "Of Experience," *The Essays of Montaigne*, tr. E. J. Trechman, Oxford University Press, New York, n.d.

12. D. Kahnemann, P. Slovic, and A. Tversky, eds., *Judgment under Uncertainty: Heuristics and Biases*, Cambridge University Press, Cambridge, 1982, pp. 3–20, 115–28, 129–52.

13. Plato *Laws*, tr. Thomas L. Pangle, Basic Books, New York, 1980, bk. 4, 716a–716b, bk. 5, 731c–731d, bk 9, 860d–864.

14. Thomas Aquinas, *Summa Theologica*, tr. Fathers of the English Dominican Province, vol. 2, Benziger Brothers, New York, 1947, question 58, art. 2, p. 1436.

15. Aristotle *Nicomachean Ethics*, tr. Martin Ostwald, Bobb-Merrill, Indianapolis, 1962, bk. 5, 1136a–1138a.

16. See Walter Burkert, *Greek Religion*, tr. J. Raffan, Harvard University Press, Cambridge, 1985, pp. 75–82, for the historical model of Plato's religious prescriptions in *Laws*.

17. Plato *Laws* bk. 9, 853d–855d.

18. Ibid., bk. 4, 777d–777e.

19. Aristotle *Nicomachean Ethics* bk. 5, 1129b. It was a mistake not lost on Aristotle's most severe critic, Hobbes, *De Cive*, ed. Sterling Lamprecht, Appleton-Century-Crofts, New York, 1946, pp. 45–46.

20. See Sigmund Freud, *Group Psychology and the Analysis of the Ego*, tr. James Strachey, Liveright, New York, 1967.

21. Aristotle *Nichomachean Ethics* bk. 4, 1119b–1121a.

22. Plato *Republic* bk. 4, 444b–445b; *Laws*, bk. 5, 728b–728e.

23. Aristotle *Nichomachean Ethics* bk. 3, 1113b–1115a, bk. 5, 1138a–1138b.

24. Augustine *City of God* pp. 112, 694–98.

25. Friedrich Nietzsche, *On the Genealogy of Morals*, tr. Walter Kaufmann, Vintage Books, New York, 1969, pp. 57–96.

26. Plato, *Gorgias*, tr. and ed. Walter Hamilton, Penguin Books, Harmondsworth, 1971, 481–522.

27. Jacqueline Scherer, "An Overview of Victimology," in *Victimization of the Weak*, ed. Jacqueline Scherer and Gary Shepherd, Charles Thomas, Springfield, Ill., 1982, pp. 8–27.

28. Gerold Mikula, "The Experience of Injustice," in *Justice in Social Relations*, ed. H. W. Bierhoff et al., Plenum Press, New York, 1986, pp. 103–23.

29. Morton Deutsch, *Distributive Justice*, Yale University Press, New Haven, 1985, pp. 46–63.

30. Faye Crosby, *Relative Deprivation and Working Women*, Oxford University Press, New York, 1982; Faye Crosby et al. "Two Rotten Apples Spoil the Justice Barrel," in *Justice in Social Relations*, ed. Bierhoff et al., pp. 267–81; Jerald Greenberg, "On the Apocryphal Nature of Inequity Distress," in *The Sense of Injustice*, ed. Robert Folger, Plenum Press, New York, 1984, pp. 167–86; Joanne Martin, "The Tolerance of Injustice," in *Relative Deprivation and Social Comparison: The Ontario Symposium*, vol. 48, ed. James Olson et al., Lawrence Erlbaum, Hillsdale, N.J., 1986, pp. 217–42, and "When Expectations and Justice Do Not Coincide: Blue-Collar Visions of a Just World," in *Justice in Social Relations*, ed. Bierhoff et al. pp. 317–35.

31. Melvin J. Lerner, *Belief in a Just World*, Plenum Press, 1980.

32. Lise Dubé and Serge Guimond, "Relative Deprivation and Social Protest: The Personal-Group Issue," in *Relative Deprivation and Social Comparison*, ed. James Olson et al., pp. 201–16; David Sears et al., "White's Opposition to Busing: Self-Interest or Symbolic Politics?" *American Politi-*

cal Science Review, 73 (1979): 369–84; and Sidney Verba and Gary R. Orren, *Equality in America*, Harvard University Press, Cambridge, 1985, pp. 248–51.

33. My remarks about Cicero are based on *The Offices*, tr. Walter Miller, Loeb Library, Harvard University Press, Cambridge, 1921, bk. 1, chaps. 7, 9, and 11, bk. 2, chap. 7.

34. Plato *Laws* bk. 9, 880b–881d.

35. These issues are taken up by Jonathan Glover, *Causing Death and Saving Lives*, Penguin Books, Harmondsworth, 1977, pp. 92–112, and by B. Williams, "A Critique of Utilitarianism," in *Utilitarianism: For and Against*, J. J. C. Smart and B. Williams, Cambridge University Press, Cambridge, 1978, pp. 93–107. They are very troubling but are not relevant to the Ciceronian notion of passive injustice, which refers only to the duties of republican citizens.

36. It is useless to speak of passive injustice in the many traditional societies that are economically and politically as impoverished as the one described by Edward C. Banfield, *The Moral Basis of a Backward Society*, Free Press, Chicago, 1963, not to mention modern dictatorships.

37. Joel Feinberg, *Harm to Others*, Princeton University Press, Princeton, N.J., 1984, pp. 126–86; and H. Goldstein, "Citizen Co-operation: The Perspective of the Police," in *The Good Samaritan and the Law*, ed. J. Ratcliffe, Anchor Books, New York, 1966, pp. 199–208.

38. Joel Feinberg, *Doing and Deserving*, pp. 3–14, and David Heyd, *Supererogation*, Cambridge University Press, Cambridge, 1982.

39. Roger Brown, *Social Psychology. The Second Edition*, Free Press, New York, 1986, pp. 43–46, 67–88; and B. Litané and J. M. Darley, *The Unresponsive Bystander*, Appleton-Century-Crofts, New York, 1970, pp. 29–36, 121–28.

40. Selma Pfeiffenberger, *The Iconography of Giotto's Virtues and Vices at Padua*, University Microfilms, Ann Arbor, 1966; Adolf Katzenellenbogen, *Allegories of the Virtues and Vices in Medieval Art*, W. W. Norton, New York, 1964, pp. 63–72; Erwin Panofsky, *Renaissance and Renascences in Western Art*, Harper & Row, New York, 1960, pp. 152–53; and Robert Smith, "Giotto: Artistic Realism, Political Realism," *Journal of Medieval History* (Amsterdam) 4 (1978): 267–84.

41. That Ciceronian passive injustice was being discussed by medieval political thinkers can be seen in the writings of Giotto's younger contemporary, Marsiglio of Padua. See, especially, Cary J. Nederman, "Knowledge, Justice and Duty in the *Defensor Pacis*: Marsiglio of Padua's

Ciceronian Impulse," an unpublished paper delivered at the 1988 annual meeting of the American Political Science Association, Washington, D.C.

42. Gal. 5:19–23.

43. *DeShaney v. Winnebago County Department of Social Services et al.*, 57 *U.S.L.W.* 4224 (February 21, 1989).

44. Aristotle *Nicomachean Ethics* bk. 7, 1149a–b, bk. 4, 1125b–1126b; and *Rhetoric*, bk. 1, 1370b, bk. 2, 1378b.

CHAPTER 2

1. *The Autobiography of Johann Wolfgang von Goethe*, vol. 1, tr. John Oxenford, University of Chicago Press, Chicago, 1974, pp. 25–26.

2. T. D. Kendrick, *The Lisbon Disaster*, Methuen, London, 1956. I have relied on this excellent work for all of my information about the events in Lisbon.

3. Voltaire, *Poem upon the Lisbon Disaster*, tr. Anthony Hecht, Perman Press, Lincoln, Mass., 1977.

4. R. A. Leigh, ed., "Rousseau à François-Marie Arouet de Voltaire," August 18, 1756, *Correspondance Complète de Rousseau*, vol. 4, Geneva, 1967, pp. 37–84.

5. "Discours sur l'origine et les fondemens de l'inégalité parmis les hommes," *Oeuvres Complètes de Jean-Jacques Rousseau, Pléiade*, vol. 3, Paris, 1964, pp. 111–223.

6. Immanuel Kant, *Werke*, ed. Ernst Cassirer, Bruno Cassirer, Berlin, 1922, vol. 1, pp. 429–84.

7. Cicero *The Offices* bk. 2, chap. 5.

8. William James, "On Some Mental Effects of the Earthquake," *Memories and Studies*, Greenwood Press, New York, 1968, pp. 212–14.

9. Vanderlyn R. Pine, "Dying, Death and Social Behavior," in *Anticipatory Grief*, ed. Bernard Schoenberg et al., Columbia University Press, New York, 1974, pp. 31–47; Stephen V. Gullo, Daniel J. Cherico, and Robert Shadick, "Suggested Stages and Response Styles in Life-threatening Illness: A Focus on the Cancer Patient," ibid., pp. 53–78; Martha Wolfenstein, *Disaster: A Psychological Essay*, Routledge & Kegan Paul, London, 1957; and Ronnie J. Bulman and Camille B. Wortman, "Attribution of Blame and Coping in the 'Real World': Severe Accident Victims React to Their Lot," *Journal of Personality and Social Psychology* 35 (1977): 351–63.

10. Kelly G. Shaver, "Defensive Attribution: Effects of Severity and Relevance on the Responsibility Assigned for an Accident," *Journal*

of Personality and Social Psychology 14 (1970): 101–13.

11. Russell R. Dynes and Daniel Yutzy, "The Religious Interpretation of Disaster," *Topic* 10 (1965): 34–48.

12. Gideon Sjoberg, "Disasters and Social Change," in *Man and Society in Disaster*, ed. George W. Baker and Dwight W. Chapman, Basic Books, New York, 1962, pp. 356–84; and Michael Barkun, *Disaster and the Millennium*, Yale University Press, New Haven, 1974, pp. 79–80.

13. Tom Nugent, *Death at Buffalo Creek*, Norton, New York, 1973, pp. 185–89. See, also, Kai Erikson, *Everything in Its Path*, Simon and Schuster, New York, 1976, esp. pp. 176–83.

14. Dynes and Yutzy, "Religious Interpretation of Disaster"; Allen H. Barton, *Communities in Disaster*, Doubleday, New York, 1969, pp. 205–73.

15. John P. Spiegel, "Cultural Variations in Attitudes toward Death and Disaster," in *The Threat of Impending Disaster*, ed. G. M. Grosser et al., MIT Press, Cambridge, 1966, pp. 283–99.

16. R. D. Abrams and J. E. Finesinger, "Guilt Reactions in Patients with Cancer," *Cancer* 6 (1953): 474–92.

17. Wolfenstein, *Disaster*, pp. 9–10, 34–35, 53–55, 158–59, and 167.

18. Edward Keyes, *Cocoanut Grove*, Atheneum, New York, 1984; and Helene R. Veltfort and George E. Lee, "The Cocoanut Grove Fire: A Study in Scapegoating," *Journal of Applied and Social Psychology* (Clinical Supplement 2) 38 (1943): 138–54.

19. Charles Fritz and H. B. Williams, "The Human Being in Disasters: A Research Perspective," *American Academy of Political Science* 109 (1957): 42–51.

20. Max Gluckman, "Moral Crises: Magical and Secular Solutions," in *The Allocation of Responsibility*, ed. Max Gluckman, Manchester University Press, Manchester, 1972, pp. 1–50.

21. Eliot A. Cohen and John Gooch, *Military Misfortune*. Manuscript to be published by the Free Press. For the general importance of hierarchy in attributing responsibility, see V. Lee Hamilton, "Who Is Responsible?: Toward a General Social Psychology of Responsibility Attribution," *Social Psychology Quarterly* 41 (1978): 316–28; and V. Lee Hamilton and Joseph Sanders, "The Effect of Roles and Deeds on Responsibility Judgments: The Normative Structure of Wrongdoing," ibid., 43 (1981): 237–54.

22. That seems to be implied in the absolving of the captain of the *Vincennes* for shooting down a civilian airplane.

23. Shulamith Firestone, *The Dialectic of Sex*, Bantam Books, New York, 1970.

24. Simone de Beauvoir, *The Second Sex*, tr. M. Parsley, Bantam Books, New York, 1961.

25. Jean-Paul Sartre, *Anti-Semite and Jew*, tr. George J. Becker, Schocken Books, New York, 1965.

26. R. Dudley Edwards and T. Desmond Williams, eds., *The Great Famine*, Brown and Nolan, Dublin, 1956; and Cecil Woodham-Smith, *The Great Hunger*, Hamish Hamilton, London, 1962.

27. Guido Calabresi and Philip Bobbitt, *Tragic Choices*, W. W. Norton, New York, 1987, pp. 151–52.

28. I owe this interpretation to Martha C. Nussbaum, *The Fragility of Goodness*, Cambridge University Press, Cambridge, 1986, pp. 51–82.

29. Kai Erikson, *Everything in Its Path*, pp. 176–83; Robert J. Lifton, "Psychological Effects of the Atom Bomb on Hiroshima: The Theme of Death," *Daedalus* 92 (1963): 462–97.

30. Michel de Montaigne, "Of the Useful and the Honest," *The Essays of Montaigne*, tr. E. J. Trechman, Oxford University Press, New York, n.d.

31. Frederick Kiefer, *Fortune and Elizabethan Tragedy*, Huntington Library, Pasadena, 1983.

32. Immanuel Kant, *Metaphysische Anfangsruende der Rechtslehre, Werke*, vol. 7, ed. Bruno Kellerman, Bruno Cassirer, Berlin, 1922, pp. 126–30; "Zum ewigen Frieden," vol. 6, pp. 417–74.

33. Michael Paul Rogin, *Fathers and Children: Andrew Jackson and the Subjugation of the American Indian*, Knopf, New York, 1975, p. 210.

34. Norman Graebner, ed., *Manifest Destiny*, Bobbs-Merrill, Indianapolis, 1968, pp. 319–21; Frederick Merk, *Manifest Destiny and Mission*, Vintage Books, New York, 1966, pp. 220–21; and Albert K. Weinberg, *Manifest Destiny*, Johns Hopkins Press, Baltimore, 1935.

35. Milton Friedman, *Capitalism and Freedom*, University of Chicago Press, Chicago, 1982, pp. 13, 23–24, 40, 112.

36. Friedrich A. Hayek, *Law, Legislation and Liberty*, vol. 2, *The Mirage of Social Justice*, University of Chicago Press, Chicago, 1976.

37. Edna Ullmann-Maragalit, "Invisible-Hand Explanations," *Synthèse* 39 (1987): 263–91, for a full account of the nature of these explanations and their relation to functionalist hypotheses.

38. Michael Oakeshott, "Rationalism in Politics" and "Political Education," in *Rationalism in Politics and Other Essays*, Basic Books, New York, 1962, pp. 1–36, 111–36, and *Of Human Conduct*, Clarendon Press, Oxford, 1975.

39. Richard Hofstadter, *Social Darwinism*, Beacon Press, Boston, 1955, pp. 50–66.

40. Milton Friedman, *Capitalism and Freedom*, pp. 110–18.

41. Robert E. Lane, "Market Justice, Political Justice," *American Political Science Review* 80 (1986): 383–402.

42. G. A. Cohen, *Karl Marx's Theory of History: A Defense*, Oxford University Press, Oxford, 1982, esp. pp. 278–96.

43. David Brion Davis, *The Fear of Conspiracy*, Cornell University Press, Ithaca, N.Y., 1971, p. xiv.

CHAPTER 3

1. Aristotle *Nicomachean Ethics* bk. 2, 1108b; and *Rhetoric* bk. 2, 1386b–87b.

2. Aristotle *Politics*, tr. Carnes Lord, University of Chicago Press, Chicago, 1984, bk. 5, 1311a–b.

3. Peter Berger, "On the Obsolescence of the Concept of Honor," *European Journal of Sociology* 9 (1970): 339–47.

4. The following remarks, unless otherwise indicated, are based upon "Discours sur l'origine et les fondemens de l'inégalité parmis les hommes," *Oeuvres Complètes de Jean-Jacques Rousseau*, vol. 3, Pléiade, Paris, 1964, pp. 111–223, esp. note 19.

5. Jean-Jacques Rousseau, *Emile*, tr. Allan Bloom, Basic Books, New York, 1979, p. 101.

6. Ibid., pp. 65–66.

7. Ibid., pp. 97–101.

8. N. Bischof, "On the Phylogeny of Human Morality," in *Morality as a Biological Phenomenon*, ed. Gunther S. Stent, University of California Press, Berkeley, 1978, pp. 61–62; Melvin Konner, *The Tangled Wing*, Harper & Row, New York, 1982, pp. 208–35; and Carol Tavris, *Anger*, Simon and Schuster, New York, 1982, pp. 31–36, 46–65.

9. Peter Blau, *Exchange and Power in Social Life*, John Wiley and Sons, New York, 1964, pp. 143–67, 227–33.

10. I owe this important point to Samuel Scheffler and Bernard Williams.

11. William Damon, "The Development of Justice and Self-Interest During Childhood," in *The Justice Motive in Social Behavior*, ed. Melvin J. Lerner and Sally C. Lerner, Plenum Press, New York, 1981, pp. 57–72; Faye Crosby and A. Miren Gonzalez-Intal, "Relative Deprivation and Eq-

uity Theories," in *The Sense of Injustice*, ed. Robert Folger, Plenum Press, New York, 1984, pp. 141–66; Jerald Greenberg, "On the Apocryphal Nature of Inequity Distress," ibid., pp. 167–86; Joanne Martin and Alan Murray, "Catalysts for Collective Violence," ibid., pp. 95–139, and "Distributive Injustice and Unfair Exchanges," in *Equity Theories: Psychological and Sociological Perspectives*, ed. David M. Messick and Karen S. Cook, Praeger, New York, 1983, pp. 169–205; and Robert Folger, "A Referent Cognitions Theory of Relative Deprivation," in *Relative Deprivation and Social Comparisons*, ed. James M. Olson et al., pp. 34–53.

12. J. G. M. Itard, *Rapport Fait à son Excellence le Ministre de l'Intérieur sur les Nouveaux Développemens et l'Etat Actuel du Sauvage de l'Auveyron*, Paris, 1807, pp. 81–82, *De l'Education d'un Homme Sauvage*, Paris, 1801, pp. 81–82, 96–97.

13. John Stuart Mill, *Utilitarianism*, J. M. Dent, London, 1944, pp. 38–49. Mill's lukewarmness toward democracy comes out most strongly in *Representative Government*, especially in the sections devoted to local government. One might also argue that for all its benevolence, utilitarianism is inherently paternalistic.

14. *Oeuvres Complètes*. Vol. 1, *Les Confessions*. Pléiade, Paris, 1959, pp. 18–20.

15. Gillead Bar-Elli and David Heyd, "Can Revenge Be Just or Otherwise Justified?" *Theoria* 52 (1986): 68–86.

16. Francis Bacon, "Of Revenge," *The Essays*, Penguin Books, Harmondsworth, 1985.

17. Robert Hogan and Nicholas P. Emler, "Retributive Justice," in *The Justice Motive in Social Behavior*, ed. Melvin J. Lerner and Sally C. Lerner, Plenum Press, New York, 1981, pp. 125–43.

18. P. S. Atiya, *Promises, Morals and Law*, Clarendon Press, Oxford, 1981, pp. 140–42.

19. Hubert J. Treston, *Poine*, Longmans, Green, London, 1923, pp. 23–94.

20. Pietro Marongui and Graeme Newman, *Vengeance*, Rowman and Littlefield, Totowa, 1987.

21. Larry McCaffery, "A Spirit of Transgression," in *E. L. Doctorow: Essays and Conversations*, ed. Richard Trenner, Ontario Review Press, Princeton, N.J., 1983, pp. 43–45; and Paul Levine, *E. L. Doctorow*, Methuen, London, 1985.

22. Jean-Paul Sartre, Preface to *The Wretched of the Earth*, by Frantz Fanon, tr. Constance Farrington, Grove Press, New York, 1963, pp. 7–26;

and Paul Wilkinson, *Terrorism and the Liberal State*, Macmillan, London, 1986, pp. 55–56, 74–77, 100.

23. Michael Walzer, "The Moral Standing of States," in *International Ethics*, ed. Charles Beitz et al., Princeton University Press, Princeton, N.J., 1985, pp. 217–36.

24. Heinz Kohut, *Self-Psychology and the Humanities*, ed. Charles B. Strozier, W. W. Norton, New York, 1985, pp. 97–160, 252–53. Kohut, in spite of disclaimers, applied the term specifically to the hero of *Michael Kohlhaas* and then to Hitler and the Palestinians in its pejorative, colloquial sense. The issue is not the place of the word *narcissism* in the psychoanalytical vocabulary but its use in politics.

25. Friedrich Nietzsche, *On the Genealogy of Morals*, tr. Walter Kaufmann, Vintage Books, New York, 1969, pp. 70–81.

26. Erwin Panofsky, *Studies in Iconology*, Harper & Row, New York, 1962, pp. 109–10 nn. 48, 49a.

27. Cicero *Offices* bk. 2, chap. 9–11.

28. Michel de Montaigne, "On Some Lines of Virgil," *The Essays*.

29. D. Kahnemann, P. Slovic, and A. Tversky, eds., *Judgment under Uncertainty: Heuristics and Biases*, Cambridge University Press, Cambridge, 1982, pp. 111–16.

30. Adam Smith, *The Theory of Moral Sentiments*, ed. D. D. Raphael and A. L. Macfie, Liberty Classics, Indianapolis, Ind. 1982, pp. 90–92.

31. Edmund Cahn, *The Sense of Injustice*, New York University Press, 1949, pp. 11–27; and Hogan and Emler, "Retributive Justice."

32. David Hume, *A Treatise of Human Nature*, ed. L. A. Selby-Brigge, Clarendon Press, Oxford, 1983, pp. 477–573.

33. James R. Kluegel and Eliot R. Smith, *Beliefs about Inequality*, De Gruyter, New York, 1986.

34. Jennifer Hochschild, *What's Fair?* Harvard University Press, Cambridge, 1981; and Sidney Verba and Gary R. Orren, *Equality in America*, Harvard University Press, Cambridge, 1985, pp. 1–51.

35. J. Stacy Adams, "Inequity in Social Exchange," in *Advances in Experimental Social Psychology*, vol. 2, ed. James M. Olson et al., Academic Press, New York, 1965, pp. 267–99; Kenneth L. Dion, "Responses to Perceived Discrimination and Relative Deprivation," ibid., pp. 159–79; and W. G. Runciman, *Relative Deprivation and Social Justice*, Routledge & Kegan Paul, London, 1966, pp. 247–95.

36. Vivien Hart, *Democracy and Distrust*, Cambridge University Press, Cambridge, 1978.

37. Robert E. Lane, "Market Justice, Political Justice," *American Political Science Review* 80 (1986): 383–402.

38. Aristotle *Politics* bk. 3, 1280a–b, bk. 4, 1295b–1297a, bk. 5, 1301a–1303a, bk. 6, 1318a–b.

39. This is clearly an argument directed against Michael Walzer's *Spheres of Justice*, Basic Books, New York, 1983, esp. pp. 26–28, 313–15, with which I disagree on almost every point.

40. See, as one example among many, the university professor Thomas R. Drew, who argued that the republican character, no less than the shared understanding and the entire social fabric of the South, adhered to and depended upon black chattel slavery, "Review of the Debate in the Virginia Legislature," in *Slavery Defended*, ed. Eric L. McKittrick, Prentice-Hall, N.J., 1963, pp. 20–33; and W. S. Jenkins, *Pro-Slavery Thought in the Old South*, University of North Carolina Press, Chapel Hill, 1935.

41. Adam Smith, *Theory of Moral Sentiments*, pp. 78–82.

42. John Kleinig, *Paternalism*, Rowman and Allanheld, Totowa, 1984, pp. 156–69.

43. Dennis F. Thompson, *Political Ethics and Public Office*, Harvard University Press, Cambridge, 1988, pp. 161–70.

44. Henry Sidgwick, *The Methods of Ethics*, Macmillan, London, 1974, pp. 243–46, 266–67.

45. Jean-Jacques Rousseau, *Du Contrat Social*, Pléiade, vol. 5, bk. 1, chaps. 6–8, bk. 2, chaps. 3 and 5.

46. George Kateb, "Remarks on the Procedures of Constitutional Democracy," in *Constitutionalism, Nomos*, vol. 20, 1979, pp. 215–37.

47. Philip Brickman et al., "Microjustice and Macrojustice" in *The Justice Motive in Social Behavior*, ed. Melvin J. Lerner and Sally C. Lerner, Plenum Press, New York, 1981, pp. 173–202; and Ronald L. Cohen, "Power and Justice in Intergroup Relations," in *Justice in Social Relations*, ed. H. W. Bierhoff et al., pp. 65–85.

INDEX